KNOWING IN MY BONES

Knowing
in my bones

RUTH FOSTER
with a Preface by Sir Alec Clegg

Adam & Charles Black · London

First published 1976

A & C Black Ltd
35 Bedford Row, London WC1R 4JH

ISBN 0 7136 1664 4 (paperback)
ISBN 0 7136 1653 9 (boards)

© 1976 Ruth Foster

Printed and bound in Great Britain by
Morrison & Gibb Ltd., London and Edinburgh

Contents

Acknowledgements

I would like to thank those who helped to bring about this book.

Peter Cox, Principal of Dartington College of Arts, suggested that I should write it, and enlisted the help of the Elmgrant Trust which provided funds to cover travel and other expenses, enabling me to carry out the interviews which, as he foresaw, contributed so much to the text.

Dr Robert Witkin, of the University of Exeter, whose book *The Intelligence of Feeling* was, and is, constantly illuminating, gave me generous and penetrating help and encouragement. I doubt whether, without this, I could have carried through. The late Christian Schiller from whom, over the years, I learnt so much, sustained me with his conviction of the importance of the subject and by his patient questions and comments. I also want to thank John Allen, Principal of the Central School of Speech and Drama, and Robin Howard, Director-General of the Contemporary Dance Trust Ltd., both of whom read and commented on the manuscript.

A. R. Stone, formerly of the West Riding, who kindled the imagination and revealed the gifts of many children and adults, discussed it with me very fully. This book owes much to him and to the many children, students, teachers, dancers and actors from whom I have learnt much.

Behind many of the developments that have taken place, leading to some of the experiences described here, lies the work of the late Rudolf Laban. He enlarged the knowledge and vision of many in a wide field of movement, and much that is fruitful has come about as a result of his teaching.

Then there are those who allowed me to interview them, and whose contributions were so lively that it has been difficult to select from so much excellent material.

I also wish to thank:

Oxford University Press, Oxford, for permission to quote from *Principles of Art* by R. G. Collingwood.

MacGibbon & Kee for permission to quote extensively from *The Empty Space* by Peter Brook.

H. M. Berg for permission to quote from *Towards a Poor Theatre* by Jerzy Grotowski, published by Methuen (Copyright © 1968 by Jerzy Grotowski and Odin Teatrets Forlag, Copenhagen).

Eyre Methuen for permission to quote from *Orghast at Persepolis* by A. C. H. Smith.

The Times for permission to quote from Irving Wardle's article of 18 June 1974.

The Juilliard School, New York, for permission to quote from 'Composing a Dance' by José Limon, which appeared in the *Juilliard Review*, Winter 1955.

Photographs: facing title page and page 36 by John V. Freeman; page 27 by Anthony Crickmay, kindly loaned by the London Contemporary Dance Theatre; pages 98, 101 and 109 from the Records of the Dartington College of Arts; Appendix sequence by Michael Taylor of Aird Taylor Associates.

Preface

When my father was a pupil teacher at the end of the last century, he introduced a new 'subject' into the curriculum of the elementary school in which he was practising: it was labelled in the log-book of the school 'marching'. To the older members of our society this kind of activity has grown into physical education and has over the years meant 'drill', gymnastics, compulsory games and swimming, and has more recently embraced dance, movement and adventure training.

Within the last two decades however there has developed a deep and significant insight into the ways in which human movement relates to feeling and affects our attitudes, behaviour and thought.

Ruth Foster from her senior position at the Department of Education and Science has herself not only seen these developments at close quarters but has been personally involved in promoting them.

To add to her understanding she has interviewed leaders in their own fields, such as Kurt Jooss, Marie Rambert, Merce Cunningham and William Gaskill, as well as a number of heads of schools and class teachers who have themselves an understanding proven by experience of the ever increasing part that movement is playing in the education we provide.

The book is scholarly and profound and should prove of value to all who are seeking to know more about the powerful forces which we cannot measure but which we 'feel in our bones' and which determine so much of what we do and the ways in which we do it.

Alec Clegg

Introduction

In an era when the development of young people is dominated by measurement, by the recording of results, and by an emphasis on material ends, there is a need to explore the nature of what happens when we move, and to think about the kind of knowing of oneself to which this leads.

All movement, unless very strictly regimented, as in military drill, has an individual expressive quality which adds a flavour to everyday actions such as walking, digging or lifting. This quality is obvious in acts of social communication. In dance and drama – where it is involved in heightened form – it is a main characteristic, and this is true of the explorations of children as well as of the performances of professional artists.

An exploration of modes of movement, the nature of their expressive quality and consequent influence on the inner life of feeling, is the subject of this book.

Much of the material consists of, or is derived from, conversations with professional dancers, choreographers, actors and directors, who are admirably clear about the processes and purposes that their work involves. As in most verbal interchanges, words are not necessarily used in logical sequence, but the conversations are vivid and immediate and embody flashes of insight which, for many artists, are come by more readily in talking than in writing. Words spoken are more fluid than the more deliberate written word.

This material is so relevant to the development of children and young people that it is juxtaposed with accounts of some of their activities and experiences, as well as with recorded discussions with some of their teachers.

Modes of movement

Everyday life

Much of what we are impelled to do is directed towards, and is concerned with, managing objects – making beds, polishing furniture, clipping the hedge, digging the garden, making a cake, putting up a shelf. In doing these jobs our actions are recognisable as characteristic (though we are unaware of this), and have an individual expressive flavour; but the impulse which prompts us to carry them out is projected in the object to which all our energy and skill are directed. We are not concerned with communication, the object shapes our behaviour and in its management our feeling impulse is contained.

If we were to reach out and grab the hand of a friend who is falling, take his weight and finally bring him back to equilibrium, the impulse to act would be discharged on him as an object. We would know him in terms of his heaviness and his bulk, and our actions would be shaped up in response to the object to be managed.

If on another occasion we were to extend a welcome to the same friend we would probably reach out, take his hand, draw him towards us and perhaps embrace him. Our feeling impulse towards him would be manifested, and reciprocated, in the quality of our expressive gestures, enabling us to recognise that we perhaps warm to him and like him more than we had expected or, on the other hand, we may realise that our actions have outrun our real feelings.

In preventing the friend from falling, our actions are adapted to him, and respond to him, as an object; in welcoming him, the initiating impulse is expressed in gestures which reciprocate our feelings enabling us to recall and recognise them.

There are experiences in which adaptation to and management of objects predominates, and others where the organisation and recognition of feeling is paramount. Neither mode is exclusive of the other; the primarily objective often carries a flavour of the expressive, and the expressive, since it involves the management of media (materials, gestures, sounds, words), may be coloured by the objective; but if the expressive mode is feebly developed the life of feeling is crippled.

But there are forms of behaviour often referred to, and mis-understood, as self-expressive, in which the process is different. For example, young girls scream and cry hysterically in a seething mass and so manifest their adulation of a pop idol. Some boys engage, as do some girls, in acts of violence and destruction. We may say that their feelings get the better of them. These are examples of outbursts in which feeling is merely got rid of, and which bring relief much as vomiting brings relief to a disturbed stomach. Such behaviour is self-intoxicating, and so recurrent; it is not a means of knowing because it is not an organisation of experience. It is important to distinguish between such outbursts and the expressive process in which the inner disturbance is shaped and recognised.

The arts

It has been shown that in everyday life disturbances may be focused on, and find their medium, in the handling of objects; or they may result in outbursts, yielding no self-knowledge; or they may be manifested in expressive action through which feeling is organised and known.[1]

The arts are concerned primarily with this latter process, with the springs of feeling and its manifestation in various media (sound, movement, words, stone, pigment). As command of a medium increases, pervading and simultaneously pervaded by the inner impulse, the resonance between them is reinforced, and the life of feeling nourished. But if attention becomes focused too persistently on the medium itself action ceases to be expressive

[1] For a full exposition of these processes see *The Intelligence of Feeling* by Robert Witkin, Heinemann

and becomes impressive; that is to say, response to the medium as object becomes dominant.

A sculptor, whose medium is likely to be intractable, demanding sheer hard labour, may become preoccupied with the material itself and lose sight of it as a means to an end. Particular materials, shapes or objects may trigger off an impulse which, as he works, is reinforced and developed, but the struggle with the medium may demand such exertion that freshness is lost and the impulse subdued.

The sculptor David Smith refreshed himself continuously by drawing because, as he wrote, 'the original creative impetus must be maintained during labour. Drawing is the fast moving search which keeps physical labour in balance'.[1]

The dancer, who must wrestle with an intractable body, faces similar problems to those of the sculptor.

If management of the medium is inadequate, the impulse, lacking sufficient means of shaping, may remain unrecognised, or feeling may overflow in self-indulgent behaviour or erupt in outbursts. In any practice of the arts there is the need to cherish the illuminating impulse as well as to nurture the means of expressing it and, in that process, knowing it.

This reciprocal process needs to be developed with delicate perception. It is essential not only to see what is happening but also to understand what that means; to provide instruction when this becomes necessary but, above all, to create an atmosphere in which the unpredictable, even the apparently impossible, can happen.

Arts in which movement is the medium

As already stated, the expressive quality of movement is inherent in all action, but is manifested in heightened form in dance, and is implicit in drama. In other arts, while movement may be the vehicle, it is not the medium (that which gives form) of expression. Stone is a medium of sculpture, pigment the medium of painting, and sound of music. The sculptor, painter and musician all use an instrument such as a chisel, brush or fiddle, and while it is true that the instrument can be considered as an extension of the

[1] *Sculpture and Writings* by David Smith, Thames & Hudson

person its use has to be mastered, and it places the artist at one remove from the medium. A musical composition is not played on the person of the performer, or a painting or sculpture made on the person of the artist, but a dance is embodied in the person of the dancer, he *is* the medium and, at the same time, the only instrument there is.

Similarly the actor, whose voice and actions embody the writer's text. The text is the *writer's* medium, but it is in the actor's person in performance, that it is made manifest.

DANCE

The dancer must develop and use rich and subtly varied resources of movement, akin to a language, but heightened, as poetry is heightened. In dance, movement takes on very closely the shape of sensation, and in turn shapes it. The experience of the dancer is an intimately personal one in which action may be said to be the very fabric of feeling itself.

In order to develop his language the professional dancer submits himself to a rigorous training in which elasticity and tireless energy, far above the needs of everyday life, have to be fought for. In pursuit of these qualities emphasis can very easily fall too heavily on technical resources so that the body is regarded more as an object than as the medium. The dancer then becomes akin to the acrobat, whose performance may be brilliantly exciting, but for whom technical perfection is the end and aim.

But, professional dancers apart, when children jump for joy, as they do, and perform other spontaneous actions expressive of their inner excitement, they experience the mode of dance. In action they *know* their excitement.

There is a further dimension to dance – the transcendent quality. In the past this has been associated in the West with religion: 'Divine ye in dancing what I shall do'.[1] In the East it is to this day similarly associated, where the dancer/actor is held to be penetrated by, or to penetrate, another power – referred to by the Balinese, according to de Zoete, as 'the other mind'. When Martha Graham writes that a dancer 'becomes in some area an athlete of God'[2] she is, I think, implying the experience of transcendence. It is a state which is also known to less remarkable dancers.

[1] From the *Hymn of Jesus* in the Apocrypha of St John
[2] From a chapter by Martha Graham entitled 'God's Athlete' in *Martha Graham* by Karl Leabo, Theatre Arts Books, New York

DRAMA

The actor, like the dancer, is in himself both instrument and medium, needing to develop not only his resources (from the acrobatic to the exquisite) but also his voice, which he must learn to root in the same breath as action.

The expressive process is, of course, similar, but the actor's mode is usually more detailed, more realistic, more prosaic than that of the dancer. It is nearer to everyday life, and the man in the street does not find it difficult to imagine himself as an actor, whereas to perform as a dancer would seem to be beyond him.

The actor must use all his resources to penetrate the situations and characters which a text presents (or which have to be evolved in an improvisation), and he must do this within a pattern of give and take with other actors – a give and take built up in action, in listening, in sound and in silence.

The quality of his own inner life of feeling is translated into the situations and characters of the play and expressed in his performance. He is very exposed. It is not surprising that those who work in the theatre feel that the actors stand up on behalf of the audience, involving themselves by proxy in feelings and situations which reveal to members of the audience also something of themselves and their world. It has been said that an audience of convicts at St Quentin gave the closest attention to a performance of *Waiting for Godot*, finding in it a reflection and revelation of their own condition. An adolescent at a performance of *Hamlet*, though not understanding the play explicitly, found his perception of the world tremendously changed by the experience, while a young man described himself as 'taken apart' by Brook's *Lear*.

Athletics — Gymnastics — High diving

Movement is also the medium of these activities, but its function is not the same as when it serves an expressive purpose. Characteristic elements in each of these sports will be described briefly, followed by an attempt to define the differences between the function of movement in the expressive arts with its function in athletics, gymnastics and high diving, and to discriminate between the kind of knowing that each makes possible.

ATHLETICS

Athletes, like dancers, submit themselves to rigorous training, but with a different end in view and, therefore, of a different kind. They are concerned to run faster, jump higher and further, and to throw further than their competitors. Their aim is to win, and their success or failure is registered by means of measurement. They practise in order to bring their skill, and to develop their stamina, to a high pitch so that when they compete their technique is at their service – in their bones.

Success is immediate and real; they get to the tape first, clear a bar at a greater height than anybody else, or see their shot, javelin, discus or hammer land beyond the rest. But apart from this material evidence they usually know during the process of running, jumping or throwing when the action feels absolutely right and this, as well as the signal of success, brings a tremendous sense of exhilaration.

An athlete himself, or the object he throws, has to get *there*.

OLYMPIC GYMNASTICS

In women's Olympic Gymnastics four categories of activity are prescribed: three involve performance on apparatus; the fourth is set on a large mat of particular dimensions, laid on the floor. All competitors must take part in all four categories.

The body becomes an object to be swung, lifted, spun, balanced, thrown into the air and manipulated with acrobatic skill. Considerable daring is demanded; indeed some of the feats are breathtaking, and the *tour de force* is a commonplace.

Patterns of action are practised over and over again in order to perfect them for competition. The technical perfection attempted is its own end, not a means of running faster, jumping higher or throwing further than the next man.

The athlete performs realistic feats in order to beat his opponents, whose immediate presence (especially in track events), has a crucial impact on his achievement. The gymnast puts everything into perfecting the pattern of a performance in which there is nothing inherently competitive. A highly competitive situation is created because marks are awarded by a panel of judges.

EDUCATIONAL GYMNASTICS

Educational gymnastics, as practised in England, is a form of movement training designed to provide opportunities for every individual, gifted or, apparently, inept, to develop unrealised powers of self-management. Suggestions initiating activity are framed in broad terms and within these there is ample opportunity for the development of individual resources. A variety of apparatus arranged in different ways is used to extend opportunity.

According to individual ability, some sequences of action may be very daring, others more restricted, and although invented sequences may be practised to a high degree of skill they do not harden into a repertoire. There is no competition.

At every level of ability versatility is worked for, and both the naturally elastic and agile, as well as the apparently clumsy and unresilient, are helped to develop their latent powers as far as possible.

Under these circumstances it is possible for each individual to understand the nature of his own efforts, his strengths and weaknesses, and to gain confidence, over a broad spectrum, in the management of himself in action.

HIGH DIVING

The actions of high divers, like those of Olympic gymnasts, are highly acrobatic, but after the take-off from the board there are no points of support for the various somersaults, twists, flexions and rotations that are performed. Height is an additional hazard.

Because after take-off there are no intermediate cues from contact with any surface (until the water is reached) the pattern of action must reside particularly intimately in kinaesthetic awareness. The body manipulates itself as an object.

As in Olympic gymnastics the technical perfection attempted is its own end, and, again as in gymnastics, while there is nothing inherently competitive in performance, marks are awarded by a panel of judges. Each dive carries a tariff mark according to difficulty, and this mark is included in the final calculation which indicates the value given to the performance. It seems that at least for some divers, pleasure in performance is decidedly secondary to the marks awarded.

Some comparisons

These athletic and acrobatic pursuits have certain elements in common:

They are all (with the exception of educational gymnastics) competitive; either directly measurable, as in athletics, or indirectly, in terms of marks awarded by judges, as in Olympic gymnastics and high diving. Winning is what matters most, and the publicity (local or national) which is attendant on success adds lustre to achievement, but also underlines what is termed 'failure', that is, not coming in first. In all these events the body is, dominantly, an object, to be moved in various ways. This is seen very clearly in Olympic gymnastics and high diving, but it is also a main factor in athletics, again seen most clearly in all forms of jumping. In field events, where an object is propelled, both body and object are one until the moment of release.

Dancers also run and leap, twist and spin, and the actors' training, too, involves a considerable degree of agility. But although there is an element of the objective attitude to the management of the body the dominant mode is expressive. In the arts, action manifests and gives form to feeling, and while feeling is of course involved in athletics and gymnastics the impulse is directed mainly towards propulsion, and through skilful propulsion to winning. It is true that in women's Olympic gymnastics certain dance-like attitudes have been introduced, often at the start or finish of an acrobatic sequence; but these attitudes remain, for the most part, no more than a simulation of expressive action.

Athletes, gymnasts and high divers know, exactly, in terms of skill, what they are about; but the more they specialise, and specialise they must, the narrower their practice becomes, and what they know of themselves in terms of their medium – movement – is similarly restricted. They submit themselves to certain patterns of action and their sensing is thus accommodated to a particular form; the *same* impulse is recalled in the *same* pattern, with the slight variations that make for success or failure. They need to master their medium, but their medium is their master. The experience in movement of dancers and actors is not only much wider, but also more subtle because of its reciprocal relationship with feeling. It is true that practice, especially for dancers, involves some repetition of certain phrases of action, but these are many and varied and should be – and usually are – rooted in, and reinforce, feeling.

In athletics and gymnastics, the energy built up by strenuous training appears to be expended; in the arts it is, in the main, created, partly because it is less dependent upon physiological efficiency than upon continuing renewal from reciprocity with the feeling impulse. There are, clearly, factors of build and temperament which impel individuals to devote themselves to certain competitive fields of action, and in so doing they feel fulfilled – when they succeed. Success strengthens the impulse to continue to submit to the ordeals involved in training and competition, and in this sense their personality is expressed. Skill is achieved, and this much they know in their bones; they also know success and failure in terms of measurement or marks. But what they know of themselves *in movement* is dominantly objective, and although intense feeling is involved it is known only through the limited and repetitive actions that an event demands.

These comparisons are made in an attempt to define the differences between the function of movement in the expressive arts with its function in athletics, gymnastics and high diving, and to discriminate between the kind of knowing that each makes possible. There is a need to do this because that which is seen to be measurable and to furnish results is apt to take precedence over other immeasurable processes, which are of crucial importance to personal development.

Knowing in my bones

It would probably be accepted that certain skills become so much a part of oneself that they are never quite forgotten (e.g. skating, swimming, typing, cycling); they are kinaesthetic patterns and although we may find ourselves out of practice we quickly feel our way back again. We know 'in our bones' what we are about.

Also 'in my bones' I know my way about my house: I know that if the fireplace is on my right the window is on the left, the change from the bare floor to the carpet locates me not far from the door. I know from its hardness, softness and shape that I am sitting on this chair and not on that, that in one I am 'on edge', and in the other relaxed. I have not mapped out the room; I have inhabited it. Over and above what I know through action (a synthesis of movement, sight, touch, hearing) the room has an atmosphere compounded of colours, shapes, sounds and previous experiences, so that it has become, perhaps, primarily a refuge or primarily a meeting place; my body is charged with, and remembers, these experiences.

It may be that presently I need to post a letter, and the distance, the slope of the hill and the time it will take are known to me, because I remember the 'feel' of the distance, of the slope, of the turning of the corner and *myself* in that situation. It is not merely a visual picture, it is 'in my bones'.

If I set out on my errand to the post I may think of the experience mainly in terms of the effort involved, yet even in a glum mood my body will vibrate to many aspects of the journey. The sound of brakes applied suddenly will explode an instantaneous tension, the shouts of children, the cawing of rooks and the bite of the wind will echo in me. I shall expand to a warm sun or a friendly wave. All these experiences vibrate in the body as, very obviously, do the rhythms of music, which are kinetically made,[1] and the gestural quality in speech.

In his *Principles of Art* Collingwood describes the Cézanne-Berenson approach to painting:

> ... the spectator's experience in looking at a picture is not a specifically visual experience at all. What he experiences does not consist of what he sees. It does not even consist of this as modified, supplemented and expurgated by the work of the visual imagination. It does not belong to sight alone, it belongs also (and on some occasions even more essentially) to touch. As his own statements abundantly show, he is thinking, or thinking in the main, of distance, space and mass; not of touch sensations, but of motor sensations such as we experience by using our muscles and moving our limbs. ... In short: what we get from looking at a picture is not merely the experience of seeing; it is also, and in Mr Berenson's opinion more importantly, the imaginary experience of certain complicated muscular movements.[2]

We forget that action underlies so much of our experience, even our concepts of near, far, high and low – concepts which are modified as our arms and legs grow longer. Our judgment of distances in the horizontal plane are much nearer the mark than those in the vertical plane because we usually move across more or less horizontal space and seldom ascend vertical height.

We are in the world through our body, and the basis of knowledge lies in sensori-motor experience, the most intimate mode of knowing. 'My body is the fabric into which all objects are woven, and it is, at least in relation to the perceived world, the general instrument of my comprehension'.[3]

[1] 'For me music is more and more an extension of the bodily functions, rather than simply a technical craft. If you're playing the clarinet you must become something that moves.' Gordon Jones – interview

[2] *The Principles of Art* by R. G. Collingwood, Oxford University Press

[3] *Phenomenology of Perception* by Merlau-Ponty, Routledge & Kegan Paul

Experience of myself

Through my body I experience the environment, I establish relationships, above all I experience myself – what it feels like to be me. This is very variable: I feel elated, sluggish, determined, idle, excited or depressed. These states are recognised by myself and others through my actions and attitudes, and my actions reinforce and change my experience of myself.

> Some days I feel very tall and can see over everybody's heads. I am me, and I want everybody to know. I feel good. Other days my eyes are on a level with other people's, and my legs are short.

> I feel different weights according to my mood. I feel strong, or fragile, or helpless, or buoyant.

> Body image suggests to me the times when image sensations are stimulated which seem to have no bearing on outside appearances, but do alter verbal and sometimes physical responses. For me these image sensations are usually connected with size and weight – because I am overweight and constantly aware of it. I feel small when I'm cold, large when I'm hot. Feeling small usually means feeling firm with my skin tight on my body and the opposite when I feel large.

These comments, made by students, show a vivid awareness of changes in what may be described as the very texture of their bodies, and thus in themselves. Such changes happen but are not induced; for some, certain experiences are associated with particular actions and situations.

> Sitting around – lectures, staffroom – feel heavy; weight seems to be in bottom, legs, it's an effort to think up – puddingy.

> Generally tend to slow down and come to an almost complete standstill if I'm with people I trust, in a safe place and I'm happy – become virtually immobile, but feel very peaceful.

I have done nothing all day, consequently I feel fat and dirty.

They are, of course, well aware of the changes brought about by different clothes – 'My whole behaviour changes if I wear trousers rather than a skirt'. Cycling, driving a car, wind, rain heights all have an impact on their feelings about themselves, of how they present themselves to themselves.

Experience of children

The function of movement in building up experience of the self begins at birth (and perhaps before birth) with the convulsive movements of the limbs and the cries which so obviously emerge from the whole body. It is generally recognised that physical contact with the mother plays a very important part in the first weeks and months. Veronica Sherborne, herself a mother of three children, who has considerable experience in working with adults and with handicapped children and adults, has said:

> Experience of the weight of the body is of first importance to the baby, who is carried and whose first experiences are of passivity, being lifted, being mobilised. All its messages are relationship ones with the mother. These are the key times for experiencing himself, and closely tied to how he is carried and manipulated. And if he can relate to this first human being, and then to siblings, and he finds he can defeat gravity by standing – if this is well done in the first years of life it is a rock, a root experience that can never be budged.
>
> When I teach people who are 18, and who are uprooted and diffuse, I have to get them back to the early experience of using the ground as a preliminary to really creative work, which comes from when a person feels as whole as possible.[1]

Gradually the baby discovers himself: he puts his hands in his mouth, his lips and tongue respond to food and make sounds; as he reaches out and grasps to bring objects to him he becomes aware of shapes and textures, discovers his own size, and in

[1] Veronica Sherborne – interview

crawling and climbing begins to perceive himself in space. The impact of his discovery of the righting reactions which, very early, give him some management of himself, and, later, his first achievement in standing upright, must be tremendous.

It happens that an adult recovering from a prolonged and serious illness has recorded his experience of standing alone for the first time:

> They used to manhandle me. But I can remember the first time I actually put my weight on my feet. It was a tremendous moment when I could say, 'Go away. Leave me. I'm here.' You could stand alone. And then you could play with that point of standing alone, to balance, and then you overbalanced, but it was nice to feel going back to the point where you were almost out of control but you could bring it back. It was *very* good.[1]

The achievement of skill certainly contributes very strongly to satisfying experiences of oneself, from the first successes in locomotion through all the antics which later become the basis for acrobatic feats (somersaults, handstands or standing on the head) – often copied from other children. The achievement of such feats, and others demanding agility, have given a surprising sense of self-satisfaction even to unathletic women students at a university.

But skill, in itself a source of self-realisation and self-satisfaction, is also used for further exploration and extension of the self. For example, when children first acquire a bicycle and achieve their balance they ride tirelessly along narrow paths, round awkward corners, up and down steep slopes extending their skill, but also becoming flying, fluid masterful creatures. The bicycles may become steeds and they themselves cowboys, or other, airborne, creatures. They are at one with their medium and are transformed in the process.

The folk dancer, Douglas Kennedy, has described how, in the course of a convivial evening drinking cider, he asked two famous potters – Leach from England and Hamada from Japan – how they made a pot. 'They both looked at me rather as through a haze, and then they began to tell me how you didn't make a pot.

[1] Leslie Read – interview

You didn't make it with your hands, and you didn't make it with your head, and eventually they looked at me and said: "You ought to know, you make it with your body".' This was reinforced by a master potter working at Wedgwood's who, when asked how, without measurements, he got the right shape, said: 'I have thirty shapes in my body'.

Watching a potter at work it is impossible not to be struck by the absorption of the man in his material; he seems to enter into it and the clay into him. Both man and clay are changed.

The same process was described many years ago by the poet Walt Whitman:

> There was a child went forth every day
> And the first object he looked upon, that object he became
> And that object became part of him for the day or for a
> certain part of the day
> Or for many years or for stretching cycles of years.[1]

This is not a fundamentally different process from the one we see in children's play where they 'become' the teacher, the doctor, or their father, or some hero from a story, thus, perhaps, coming to terms with tense situations, trying themselves out in different ways, extending their idea of themselves.

The impact of particular forms of movement on self-awareness

We never want to be tied down to fixed feelings about ourselves; comments and encounters involve *reactions* and in these we are changed, though we have little control over the process. But by changes of clothing (which by weight, texture and cut modify stance and action), by doing acrobatics and by dancing we intentionally explore, and experience, changes in our feelings for ourselves. This is especially noticeable in dance and it takes a dancer to understand and describe the process:

> The most finest way of the arts to try to find that inward
> self-image, that kinaesthetic thing of knowing, awareness,
> simply physical awareness, then begins to feed back and give

[1] From *Leaves of Grass*

some kind of image and feeling of *who* you are and *what* you are; and it is the struggle to find that, that every dancer who is intelligently interested in what they are doing does always try to find; and works at it. And I think if you feel you have danced well it's a kind of having that internal sense of who you are. Not that you can put it into words, as we were saying, and it may be different for you at different times, but somehow things begin to make sense. And you sense this in some dancers, in the way they move; you can't think why your eyes go to them, but it's probably for the reason that they have this tremendously strong self-image.[1]

The contribution of dance to the development of self-awareness is described by the headmaster of a secondary school housed in a grim building in an industrial city. A young and gifted teacher had introduced dance throughout the school:

Something very important is happening to the girls, though I don't quite know what it is, but it certainly must involve a discovery of personal powers. Young people, as we know, do not form a self-concept rationally; they do it in all sorts of affective ways – intuitive responses to people, to situations, to themselves. Many of the children who are written off have gifts that are to do with feeling, they're to do with the self-concept. I think that this aspect of self-esteem, self-concept, the discovery of uniqueness is an important feature, and it's one that can, perhaps, be more readily achieved in dance than in most other areas.[2]

Certainly the poise, confidence and involvement of these girls was very remarkable, and it was clear that, in some of their solos, they had penetrated some of their own problems, but without any symptoms of self-indulgence.

A teacher in a primary school in a very poor district described the changes in an aggressive boy who 'shouted at people in the street, threw stones at windows; he was a real menace.' It happened that experience in movement was an important element in the school and the boy turned out to be a natural and gifted dancer. 'There was no getting away from it, he was

[1] Dan Wagoner – interview   [2] Ernest Goodman – interview

wonderful. When he was dancing he was a different person, his face and everything about him changed'.[1]

In this medium the boy seemed to find himself and gradually his aggression disappeared. Where he had been rejected by the other children he was accepted as a leader, and his other considerable abilities, including speaking and writing, began to appear. After school he would take every opportunity to dance alone in the hall. This was much more than the sheer activity of an energetic boy; he had found in expressive movement a means of manifesting to himself, and coming to terms with, the tensions which formerly had erupted in violent behaviour.

The actions of throwing stones and of shouting had merely been used to get rid of his disturbances and were senseless reactions which built up in him again and again. His behaviour was self-reactive. When he found himself in school (where, of course, there were many things to influence him), he began to be aware of his powers of movement; he no longer needed merely to get rid of his disturbances, but could incorporate them through the medium of movement. In knowing his inner being through action he began to transform himself.

What this boy had been was made very clear when, later, a situation arose where an agitator was needed to stir a crowd to action. He seized the opportunity and delivered an explosive tirade – but this behaviour had by then become understood by him as an 'act' and was no longer menacing.

In this same school, in the course of an exploration (not a production) of *The Pied Piper*, the Mayor and Corporation, having decided at a meeting not to employ the Piper to get rid of the rats, left the council chamber (a circle of chairs) and walked as a body through the street of waiting parents who stood, silent and still. One small boy (also a councillor) stayed behind to rearrange the chairs, he thus became separated from the main body and walked alone between the parents. Where the group of councillors had seemed unapproachable, the single one was not, and the parents reached out to him with pleading and demanding gestures. He could use what he 'knew' to realise that he dared not look at them and walked on, fully aware, but not turning to left or right.

[1] Bessie Bullough – interview

This solid, practical nine year old, for whom it was characteristic to stay and straighten the chairs, could not, in the ordinary way, know that in this situation it would be impossible to look the parents in the eye. And yet he seemed to know. How could this come about? In his short life he would have caught the flavour of various relationships in the adults about him – through their gestures and the sound of their voices – and furnished as he was, like the other children in the class, with a fine perception and response in movement, he was able, in action, to incorporate previous, but not recognised experiences, and to understand the situation in his bones.

The teacher who gave the boy this opportunity was a class teacher, working with the children in all 'subjects' – it would be nearer the mark to say 'media'. Asked if she thought that movement played an important part in changing children's experience of *themselves*, she said: 'I believe so firmly that it does because I've seen it happen so often. At first they may be awkward and embarrassed, but by the time they have had some experience and have become involved (it's becoming involved that is important), once you come out of that experience, which may last only a few seconds at first, there is a difference. The longer the periods of involvement, the further you go from being that awkward thing and the nearer you are to becoming *yourself*. When you get all the different beings that you *can* feel you gradually build up your own self because you know (not consciously) that you are capable of being these things; therefore you can be yourself'.[1]

Everyday experience

In everyday life the ways in which we act and react are essentially part and parcel of what it feels like to be me. Maybe I am rebuked, and I may accept the reasons for that rebuke, but beyond this acceptance it is as though my flesh and bones had congealed, and the self that I feel myself to be is experienced in the whole fabric of my body. If, on the contrary, I receive warm praise, even if, on consideration, it seems undeserved, I expand, I experience a thrill and I feel a different person. My responses are

[1] Bessie Bullough – interview

not merely with my 'mind', but with my blood and bones.

A young man, shocked by a crisis, felt himself immediately as a skeleton with the flesh hanging from his bones like old clothes. 'I knew then, and since then have always known, what it will be like to be an old man'. He not only felt, but *knew* his feelings.

Attitude

That which we know in our bones is part of the very fabric of our being; in our attitudes we unconsciously reveal something of this to the world. We use the term to denote recognition of inner states disclosed in stance, gesture and locomotion.

Remy Charlip, the American choreographer, emphasises the depth of the relationship between the outward manifestation that we refer to as attitude, and the inner life of the individual:

> To change the bodily habits is very hard work. Often it means changing one's attitude, or changing one's life, and that's a very hard thing to do. People who do it are very brave.[1]

An example of the relationship between action and inner feeling was observed by Ernest Goodman, the headmaster quoted on page 18.

> There was a whole group of disaffected girls in the Middle School, many with very serious home problems. They were problem girls; I don't mean that they were vicious, they were disaffected, and the change in attitude was remarkable in quite a short space of time. I'm convinced it came from their dance. They began to be more co-operative, they wanted to be involved in all sorts of ways, and they became gentler people. I detected a new sensitivity.[2]

The headmaster was of course aware that the change lay not only in the introduction of dance, taught with great skill and understanding, but also with the concern of the teacher for every individual.

When we say, 'I do not like his attitude', our response stems from the implicit recognition of feelings expressed in actions

[1] Remy Charlip – interview   [2] Ernest Goodman – interview

that recall similar experiences of our own. We know what the actions of others stand for.

Gestures that have a threatening or thrusting impact invite responses of attack, retreat or defence, and may well set up barriers to further communication. Gestures that have a scattering quality disperse attention, and a teacher or speaker who has a habit of this kind infects the group he is addressing and fails to recognise the source of their distraction. The open gestures of a loving parent, close friend or generous hostess create a welcome and invite further communication.

A baby responds to changes in an adult's attitude transmitted through the way in which he is handled; the quality of tension or of serenity in the adult is conveyed through touch and through sound. Later, young children are quick to respond to the moods of adults, conveyed not merely through words but also through the quality of actions. While wary teachers may recognise symptoms of discontent and rebellion they may perhaps fail to realise how instantaneously their pupils also recognise and respond to the current, as well as the more permanent, attitudes of their teachers. A teacher who is nervous (for example, under inspection), communicates his uneasiness to the class; the children may be trying hard, but their response is disturbed even though they do not recognise the cause.

An interviewer (prospective employer, or doctor) unconsciously creates a barrier if, when he receives a client, he sits with his arms folded and his legs crossed, and only moves to take notes. At the very least the visitor, who is already at a disadvantage in having to make the approach, is likely to become wary or defensive.

There are others who deliberately use stance and gesture to create particular situations. For example, the headmaster who when addressing the school insists on a high platform, makes a 'dignified' entrance and speaks from behind some sort of lectern, deliberately builds up a sense of occasion – as he sees it. The headmaster who sits behind a desk to receive his staff, pupils or parents creates, perhaps unconsciously, one kind of situation; the headmaster who has no desk in his room, who joins his visitor and invites him to sit in a comfortable chair, knows very well what he is about and sets up a situation where communication is easily possible.

It is very important for communication to understand that, whether we like it or not, we reverberate to the attitudes of others and, in turn, set up reverberations in others. We need to learn to be aware of the quality of our own attitudes – defensive, provocative or protective – and to recognise their impact on others, whether they are received and reciprocated, or rejected.

> Unless you are sensitive yourself and are sensitive to your feeling for your own movement, can you perceive accurately the significance of the movement of others? At the level of this depth of communication, which is the very basis of interpersonal relations, you have to have sensitivity and understanding of what is, on the surface, physical, but to my mind goes into depth, into the inner being of which this is part of the expression.[1]

Actors and dancers are acutely sensitive to the cues they receive from each other's attitudes, and this awareness has much to do with clarity and subtlety of communication. It is something that others need to learn to take into account. An attitude that under-lies what is said may give the lie to, or reinforce, the words spoken. This is too seldom discerned.

It is possible, by means of movement, to change attitude. We do this ourselves when, beset by tension, we decide to 'relax', or we 'face up to a difficulty', 'shrug it off', or 'stop dithering'. These are everyday usages, but there is also a game, played in twos where one is the interviewer, in the strong position, the other the client, in a vulnerable one. The interviewer adopts an attitude full of force and pressure, the client is light in tension, and tentative. There is no script, but as they talk they must gradually exchange their qualities of action; as their attitude changes the dialogue also changes and they find that the tables have turned.

It is also possible to modify the attitude of a group through movement. On one occasion a group of students arrived in an apparently exhausted and depressed state, and certainly reluctant to work. It would have been possible to send them away, or let

[1] C. J. Gill – interview

them lie down and yield to their heaviness. Instead they were asked to move calmly – which they interpreted as moving slowly but not heavily, and quietly with a gentle lightness. Gradually they changed and appeared to become refreshed. When this calm mood had been established two or three were asked to try to disturb the rest, who were to resist the disturbance if they could. The disturbers chose to be sudden, noisy and aggressive (without touching) in both action and sound. For the most part the calm group was able to remain quiet and unhurried. At the end of some fifty minutes the attitude of the whole group had changed, it was no longer depressed but alive and refreshed.

Another explicit use of movement to awake attitude was on an occasion when a group of teachers were working on the theme of Orpheus and Eurydice. It had not been too difficult to create the inhabitants of the Underworld and their antagonism to Orpheus, but to enter the state of the Blessed Spirits in their Eternity had become a problem. The group moved out from a dim indoor space on to the open roof under a high, blue sky, and there concerned themselves, separately and individually, with Timelessness and Space. There was utter quiet, and little ostensible movement. Time stood still. It is difficult to know how long this contemplative state continued, but out of the experience it became possible, at a later session, for the group to become the Blessed Spirits in Eternity. This experience so lit up one man (a footballer and cricketer) that he returned to his boys' school where he had already started work of an expressive kind and went ahead to develop movement of a superb quality – both athletic and poetic – with his boys.

The impact of various cultures

An American dancer who has studied not only the style of Martha Graham but also, in India, the style known as Bharatnatyam has described her experience when preparing to perform in the Eastern style:

> It starts about two weeks before a concert (Bharatnatyam)
> and I'm afraid that my friends feel that I am very
> unfriendly. I am not at all American, and in a very strange

way I cease to be European in attitudes about things, and even in the way I move. Interestingly all Europeans who have studied Indian dance have changed their names. I alone remain Georgia Cushman. To put it negatively, one is not sure of oneself to dabble round with name changing and image changing.[1]

Dance epitomises, as it were, the very different attitudes that belong respectively to American and Indian cultures – differences in modes of moving, of dressing and of behaviour to others. Although an individual experiences his own feelings for himself he does so in the context of an American, Indian, Italian or French culture. Sitting in the piazza of a small Italian town during a holiday it seemed easy to discern, from their modes of action, the different nationalities, and to check judgment when a group came near enough for their language to be heard.

One of the pleasures that an Englishman may enjoy in visiting, say, the United States, France or Italy, is that he begins to be infected by other modes of behaviour. He feels like a different person. This is particularly noticeable when he returns from the USA having been exhilarated by the extrovert and lively attitudes of the Americans. For a few weeks the infection is very noticeable; later, traces remain but are no longer obvious.

Ritual

Clearly defined attitudes and gestures are inherent in all ritual, because they must embody the corporate feelings of all those present, not only the leading figures but the whole community, congregation, crowd or audience. Modes and patterns of locomotion (e.g. processions), acts of blessing, of reverence, submission or exultation; ceremonial giving and receiving (of colours, orders, prizes, medals, degrees), have a specificity and clarity which makes it possible for all to follow and to share in the occasion. Expressive acts performed in common are characteristic of all ritual, but when the original impulse that gave rise to it is lost the form becomes mechanical and no longer stirs the response which makes sharing possible.

[1] Georgia Cushman – interview

Dance

Ye who dance not know not what we are knowing.[1]

Being above oneself might be said to be the origin of the impulse to dance – whether it is a child who jumps up and down with excitement, a couple in love who need in dance to go beyond words and to manifest clearly their feelings for each other, or the brief outburst of the English rugger players when the final whistle blew and they had, unusually, beaten the Welsh at Cardiff. When the 1939–45 war ended a little hairdresser in Leeds related how, in her suburb, they all (not merely the children) had run races, lit a bonfire and danced round it. She didn't know why. 'We aren't strangers any more,' she said. 'When we go to catch the tram we say "good-morning" to each other.'

On such occasions of excitement, and without any technique, people express their feelings in exuberant action, and in so doing sharpen and deepen them. *Anybody* can dance when he is deeply moved, and in so doing he knows himself, and the experience that has so moved him.

Douglas Kennedy, the folk dancer, who understands so well why people dance, referred to:

> That rhythmical process that we find very hard to describe, but which we recognize at once as an expression of vibrating life. Your reaction to the thing is not intellectually, or with any kind of critical faculty, but primarily because of the sense that it gives you of being alive in a living world.[2]

[1] From the *Hymn of Jesus* in the Apocrypha of St John
[2] Douglas Kennedy – interview

While professional dancers must develop rich resources to meet the demanding conditions of exposure to an audience, they also are very much aware of the source of dance in vitality, and of the sense that it brings to them of being fully alive.

From the field of Classical Ballet:

> Isn't it vitality above all? It is the strength of living. I don't know what else to call it.[1]

From Germany:

> A dance is a thanksgiving for what we experience as life; it's a kind of festive, almost concentration, of the possibilities and circumstances of life.[2]

From the USA, a former, notable, Graham dancer:

> This curious thing which is dance, this kind of buoyancy, or steady thrust of energy that carries the body on in some sort of urgent, or ecstatic or impassioned way.[3]

And from an American choreographer and dancer:

> When I said energy it doesn't always mean the *high* energy, but it's the release of energy. This simply goes back to the idea of being sensitized and alive physically so that you are aware of the energy release, and by that care and awareness a physical awareness which lends a vitality.[4]

The term 'energy', and certainly the adjective 'energetic', has a strong flavour of mere forcefulness and even busy-ness about it, and 'vitality' may smack of the high kicking of a line of chorus girls, but Dan Wagoner says: 'It doesn't always mean the *high* energy,' and relates it to 'the idea of being sensitized and alive'. Not mundane, but above oneself, more open, more aware. Jooss and Rambert emphasise the experience of being fully alive, and Kennedy refers to our reaction and recognition of dance 'as an expression of vibrating life' and 'the sense that it gives you of being alive in a living world'.

We see, in children, those outbursts of exuberant action in which dance has its roots. When they spot a source of pleasure and excitement they hop up and down whirling their arms, and

[1] Marie Rambert – interview
[2] Kurt Jooss – interview
[3] Jane Dudley – interview
[4] Dan Wagoner – interview

move excitedly. Even with no particular focus to their pleasure they seldom move along soberly but break out, superabundantly, impulsively, into antics of all kinds. This overflow of energy which is essential to the growth of young creatures is recognised as a sign that they are fully alive, and we say: 'They are enjoying themselves', perhaps not realising how true this is – 'them*selves*'. It is indeed a mode of knowing.

In the opening phrases of her autobiography Marie Rambert describes her early childhood:

> Movement, perpetual movement was my element. I crawled very fast on all fours, I ran very fast on all twos, I stood on my head, kicking the while for more fun. Ludwika, my nurse, used to call me 'Quicksilver', and when I was old enough to climb trees I was nicknamed 'Squirrel'. When I wasn't doing anything else I turned cartwheels.[1]

In an interview she added: 'I had an inborn, not only sense of movement, but a need of movement, a terrible need of movement. Ultimately it was all channelled into dancing'.

Merce Cunningham, the great American dancer and choreographer, is very aware of the source of dance in children's antics:

> I watched some kids out of the window once – I was teaching at Boulder, Colorado – and I was sitting drinking my coffee – they were little children, five and six years old. They were running, and skipping and suddenly I thought 'They're dancing'. There wasn't any music. They were having such a beautiful time. *Field Dances* came from that because I could see that they were running and skipping and to me it was dancing; but for them it wasn't different.[2]

The experience of the dancer

To dance is to discover – especially oneself, whether it is the boy referred to on page 19 – 'When he was dancing he was a different person' – or the dancer and choreographer, Kurt Jooss – 'Dancing is something quite special. I think it is that one becomes aware of what one is'. He describes the process:

[1] *Quicksilver* by Marie Rambert, Macmillan
[2] Merce Cunningham – interview

> Each body movement is preceded by an inner movement,
> a psychic movement, and each psychic movement is
> somehow bound to a bodily tension or movement.
> Expressive dance is not to dance and make suffering faces,
> but expressive dance is just that – to move in harmony
> with the inner movement and to have the inner movement
> brought out by the body movement. Sometimes I try to
> explain to people that it goes both ways.[1]

That it goes both ways is something that we all experience, but perhaps do not recognise. We admit that action may emerge from feeling and from idea, but not that the inner impulse is in turn modified or reinforced by action.

> When I began to explore myself physically and technically
> as a dancer I had to explore deeper and there was no
> dividing the physical and the spiritual. One could only
> call it the whole thing.[2]

And Merce Cunningham: 'It's so suddenly illuminating in some way that you don't get any other way'.[3]

These are the observations of great dancers and choreographers with all their resources of imagination and technique and their considerable experience; but the same sort of understanding of the experience of dance is expressed by a fifteen year old schoolgirl:

> I dance because it is an excellent way of describing how you
> feel, which is not possible in any other way. I find it an
> easier way of communicating with people. I tend to
> express things in much more detail, finding every aspect of
> it. Dancing makes you think more deeply about what you
> are doing. You seem to be able to get lost in a world of
> your own.

The nature of dance movement is easily recognised when, at the end of a dance, after a moment of stillness, the dancer moves away. In the course of the dance there will probably have been other moments of stillness followed by action (possibly walking or running), and no observer will have made the mistake of supposing that the dance had ended. They will also recognise

[1] Kurt Jooss – interview   [2] Dan Wagoner – interview
[3] Merce Cunningham – interview

that the movement following the final stillness (it may well be walking or running) is no longer dance. This experience illuminates something of the nature of dance. There is nothing 'fancy' about the walking or running of a dancer during a dance, the difference lies in the focus of attention, the total absorption of the inner impulse in the outer action. This disappears when the dance is over and everyday movement takes over.

The difference between dance and non-dance can also be recognised in the middle of a composition. Parents watching their schoolgirl daughters in a group dance said of one, with amazement, 'She's not dancing'. They were right; the girl in question was going through the same motions as the others, but though her actions were similar her attention was outward and diffused; there was no reciprocation between impulse and medium. Since the other dancers were totally involved her non-dancing stood out and was recognised at once by the audience.

Movement is both the medium and the content of dance

There is no story, no literary content in social dance. Folk dances, even by visiting groups from Eastern Europe who are often seen performing on television with considerable virtuosity, convey their meaning through the patterns and modes of movement – leaping, twirling, linking in chains, circling, advancing and retreating. We get the message, because even with our own limited abilities in movement we are able, in our bones, to share something of the experiences of the dancers. We also recognise what our own less spectacular and (save in the Morris) dynamically quieter folk dances stand for, with their pattern of relationships – hands joined in a circle, ranks advancing, groups interweaving, couples turning.

It is true that many Classical ballets are tied very closely to a story (e.g. *Sleeping Beauty*), while others (e.g. *Symphonic Variations*) are not, but there are many American choreographers who, although they may give a title to a work, reject attempts to attach a literary meaning to their patterns of action, much as

musicians resent attempts to describe music (other than programme music) in verbal forms.

> Basically dance is another language, a language that springs
> and comes entirely out of another place than the literary
> thing. Too often we try to reduce it to literature, and
> that's not what it is. And I think we do that because we feel
> safer with labels. From the time we are small we say: 'What's
> that?' And they say: 'It's a thingummybob', and we say,
> 'Ah, yes,' and we feel much better because we are
> conditioned to do that. And then with some people one
> can begin to look at movement and not try to translate
> everything and say 'What does it mean? Why did you do
> that?' But just look, and respond if possible. You have to
> throw out all the preconceived understanding that you
> have, and let this other thing happen.[1]

This is an important statement underlining, as it does, our
compulsion to label our experiences and to tick off items of
information, and emphasising our failure to be open and 'let
the other thing happen'. So often it is the flicker that we just
catch in the corner of our eye, as it were, which is the source of
illumination, rather than that on which we have focused.

A similar point of view emerges in a conversation with Merce
Cunningham:

> I think that it's great that in dancing you can do all those
> things about skill, about virtuosity, and yet what a dancer
> does goes beyond that. It's so suddenly illuminating in
> some way that you don't get any other way. This kind of
> thing can happen haphazardly with, say, a slap in the face,
> but in dancing it happens *that* way, and you can think that
> that is its great point. And with all the hard work we have
> to do when *that* happens anybody gets it. Skilled or
> unskilled, knowing nothing about dancing, they open
> themselves to it, even though they don't get it. That's the
> trouble; we receive this incredible thing, and immediately
> we examine it and ruin it. That's one of the terrible things
> about the mind.

[1] Dan Wagoner – interview

He, and many other American choreographers, are concerned that movement should speak for itself, as music speaks for *itself*, and they know that because every human being has experience of movement and knows 'in his bones', an audience can be expected to respond without the reinforcement of a story.

> I know meanings come out to different members of the audience varying according to what they see and what they feel. I prefer this to happen like that, for individuals, rather than my saying it should be this way, and you should feel this. It makes it difficult sometimes for my dancers because, while I can be expressive, if I think it's getting into the meaning thing I back off, probably more than is necessary. Because I've seen so often that they *seize* on meaning, and then work at that, rather than trying to see a whole thing and not a little part. It's like a handle, and they grab onto that.

Most dance compositions are given a title – and these can vary from *Clytemnestra* (Graham), based on the myth, but a highly symbolic version of it, to *Moves* (Jerome Robbins), a title which stands exactly for what the composition is about (it is un-accompanied).

The process of composition

> One must go to the studio, perhaps just start walking in a circle, and just walk, and maybe for the first day you'll do nothing but walk. And then the second day you might run a little. But you can start. Or you may go to the studio and the sun may be shining a little through the window in a particular place that's very warm, and it feels good on the feet. And that place in a space can become a very important place in which to stand, and later you, even when the sun has gone from that space, even when you've gone from that space, you may have chosen that relative point within any corresponding space as an important place to start a movement, and you may even forget later on why there was that spot you stood in. But accidents like that help me

along: and I think the main thing is to open oneself up to whatever happens, and sometimes if you do have an idea, even yielding and giving in to that idea somewhat and letting the piece take life from the movement. I think that the activity is important, the doing.[1]

This expresses very clearly the basic process in composition – exploration in the medium itself, in movement – which is also how children function. It is not the only starting point for this choreographer, but whatever germ of an idea he might start from (in his duet to the final 'Remember Me' from Purcell's *Dido and Aeneas* the words and music must have been a very important element) the exploration must be in the medium itself.

Cranes, choreographed and danced by Janet Smith, followed a process of composition very similar in kind to that described by Dan Wagoner. Unusually for her, music gave the initial impetus – a piece of recorded music by Goro Yamaguchi playing the Japanese flute. Listening to this she found that she had started to move with it, and that it seemed to pull in two opposite directions. Then, looking at the sleeve, she discovered that the longer, descriptive title to the piece was 'Depicting the joy of the young cranes leaving the nest, and the sorrow of the parents'. This explained the opposing pulls in the music of which she had been aware when she first listened to it.

The dance is delicate in quality, yet of tensile strength; it lasts only four minutes, but seems timeless, and although the dancer moves no more than two yards forwards, and retreats the same distance to her starting point it creates a great sense of space.

She describes how she went on after listening to the music:

The next thing I did was to take myself off into a space and start tinkering about, just playing with movement, first of all with the music and then without it. And the first thing that happened came almost immediately. I found myself balancing on one leg, and listening to the shifts that went on inside my body, the little adjustments that go on minutely all the time to maintain balance. This had the kind of tenuity that the flute had, the same quality. I wanted to find the same thing in movement; it excited me to listen to it.[2]

[1] Dan Wagoner – interview   [2] Janet Smith – tape recording

'The first thing that *happened*.' 'I *found* myself balancing on one leg.' So not planned, but found and recognised – 'Listening to the shifts that went on minutely inside my body'. These statements are very close to Dan Wagoner's, 'I think the main thing is to open up oneself to whatever happens – letting the piece take life from the movement.' (See page 34.) Similarly Jane Howell's 'a state of hopeful expectancy, without any strain; when everything is together and prepared, and ready to accept something – when it chooses to come'. (See page 69.)

Next:

I worked on the balancing, and went from balances on one leg to balances on two legs, and very, very little movement; but all the time not fighting for a balance, not maintaining a stillness by gripping anywhere, but letting all the tiny shifts go on, and feeling and listening to them. So the focus there was very much inside.

In performance the balances seemed quietly inevitable, with no sense whatever of struggle or unsteadiness, and reminiscent of Martha Graham's statement on one of the attributes of a dancer – 'He does not choose to fall'.[1]

Then I went back to the music, and the idea that had strongly communicated itself to me of the young cranes leaving the nest and the sorrow of the parents. From that I took two sections into this dance.

First the leaving. I began backstage and to one side, and I worked on a diagonal, just moving forward very slowly all the time to a point not more than two yards away. Throughout that movement, through the balances, I had an outward focus upwards to the diagonal that I was moving towards. I had the image in my mind of the joy of the young cranes, and this allowed me to open up the body in those balancing steps – travelling forwards, upwards, outwards – releasing all the time.

Then the second section. I simply moved, very slowly, back on the same diagonal that I had left, but very much closing in, returning in, in the body. And the image during that part was the sorrow of the parents.[2]

[1] Martha Graham in *This I Believe*, edited by Edward R. Murrow, New York   [2] Janet Smith – tape recording

There is nothing imitative in this composition; Janet Smith had not studied cranes, and had never seen one move. Neither is she telling a story 'other than for myself'. The upward diagonal *became*, and stood for, the joy of the young cranes, just as the return to the starting point became, and stood for, the sorrow of the parents. As Jooss said (see page 30), 'Expressive dance is not to dance and make suffering faces, but expressive dance is just that – to move in harmony with the inner movement and to have the inner movement brought out by the body movement'.

Janet Smith continued:

I introduced two stillnesses. One happened at the end of the going out, and it was very much the joy of the young. I have a stillness there, in the most opened and outward movement, in which I felt that I was flying. In that stillness (very slowly, the whole thing takes so much time), I very slowly shift from being that thing moving out to watching that thing that has moved out. When I come out of that stillness I am the parent returning. Still with the same balancing movements I am softening, coming down, retreating. Exactly the same movements, but the picture changes the way the balance happens in my body.

Half way back I have another stillness which is the most closed moment in the dance. It's a balance on one leg where I am very slowly preparing to rest the other foot on the knee of the supporting leg. I curl up, I tuck everything in, arms, head, shoulders; it's curled in, it's rounded, it's cocooned.

That's quite a long balance, going with, not fighting, the thing of balance. Then I continue moving backwards, turning round, turning away from the outward focus that I had moved towards. Turning away, turning away, and then, very slowly I take just the head (this is the only other movement of one specific part), just the head, very slowly through the water, turning around to look at that outward focus. Then the rest of the body is moving again, and I am very slowly turning back, and as the music finishes I'm still with its finishing.

I went *with* the music at only two points. I think that these were just two highlighting moments, because the whole movement is very general. I am not concentrating on, for example, just a finger, but on every little part as it happens. Because of that I wanted to have some moments when little, minute things happened, with nothing else moving, and one of these was to a trill of the flute, and in a position which was otherwise in stillness I just trilled with my toes.

Another part of the music that I could not not respond to was a kind of sighing climbdown that the flute makes. I had reached a point of extension of one leg and both arms outwards into the air, and to this sighing, this climbdown, I had to let my body fall very gently – a coming down. There again I was completely going with the sound.

These are the only two points where I move *with* the music.

The dance hasn't changed at all in form, yet it changes all the time. It's a difficult dance, I do have to work very much on the focus, having the images in mind, and allowing the balance to happen – if it will.

When it works, when I really put my concentration into it so that I've got the feeling of long time, of no sense of time, so that I have to snap out of it at the end – these are the times when it communicates to the fullest.

When *I'm* there, *it's* there.

Merce Cunningham's *Walkaround Time* had its original impetus from the artist Jasper Johns' suggestion that Marcel Duchamp's painting *Large Glass* would make a marvellous set for a dance, and he asked Merce Cunningham if he would be interested. 'Yes, of course,' and there and then, in Duchamp's flat, the suggestion was agreed.

Cunningham described how he went to work:

I began to think about Duchamp and what the set would be. It later came out that there were to be seven cube-shaped pieces on the stage, but up to the day of the first performance I didn't really know the size of those things, or where they were going to stand on the stage.

   They were also going to be transparent so that you could see through them. So that started that way.[1]

Cunningham went on to consider Duchamp's work and various elements in his life.

And then I began to think about movement, and I tried out some simple things. I tried out very, very, slow things; nothing relating to previous notions, just movement ideas. I decided to make it very long, a long piece divided into two parts. There would be an entracte in the middle. I put in lots of things about Duchamp and his work which I never tell anybody because this confuses people. Like ready-mades, for instance, because a ready-made is something that is already done, and you can re-use it. So the piece has things that appear, not often, but over again, and at the first performance, in the second half when we started to re-do some of the things, a little boy in the audience said: 'Look, they're doing re-runs'. All those things, but not specific in any sense. I placed a kind of striptease in this, but that's because of Marcel's *Nude Descending the Staircase*. All those things that have been in his life, but not to imitate them; they always come out as movement things, not as ideas *about* movement.

Then he described the very first stages with the dancers:

I went into a studio and I wanted to – I didn't want, I just did it. I asked one of the dancers to do a back fall, and I showed her something about it, but I let her find it for herself; then I asked one of the men to fall over her, and I asked another girl to fall over them. Then that didn't quite work, but that was because I hadn't explained it quite clearly. But I could see and said: 'Sandra, don't fall *that* way, fall the other way so that you can see where you're going'. That was *one* thing; I didn't continue from there. Then I went away and made something with two other dancers. I also wanted to put in a kind of continuing thing for Carolyn Brown, particularly in the second half. I

[1] Merce Cunningham – interview

suppose I was thinking of Duchamp's interests, but not at all
'This is meant to be. . . .'

The main thing, I think, is the tempo. Marcel always
gave one the sense of a human being who is ever calm, a
person with an extraordinary sense of calmness, as though
days could go by, and minutes could go by. And I wanted
to see if I could get that – the sense of time.

This is not, of course, a full description of the whole process of
composition, but certain important elements emerge. In the first
place, several people were gathered for dinner in Duchamp's
flat – Merce Cunningham, Jasper Johns, the artist, who was also
the designer for Cunningham's choreography, and John Cage,
the composer, who was playing chess with Duchamp's wife. The
suggestion for the composition came from Jasper Johns, arising
from a painting by Duchamp, and it was in terms of a set for a
dance, and this set emerged as seven, transparent, cube-shaped
pieces, though their size and location were not known until the
day of the first performance.

Then there was the period of thinking about the painter, his
experiences, his gifts, his nature, and a few try-outs without the
company. Then the decision about the total shape and after that
the beginning with the company – in action. Always at the back
of his head was his understanding of Duchamp and his activities
but never, in action, the statement, 'This is meant to be. . . .'
There is also the recognition by the small boy of the 're-runs',
which stood for Duchamp's ready-mades. This took place in the
second half of a long piece, which is very far from obvious, and
showed that a child, at least, could tune in to the action.

José Limon, the American dancer and choreographer wrote an
article on 'Composing a Dance'[1], using his experience in composing *The Traitor*, which was based on the tragedy of Judas Iscariot.
He described how he lived with the idea for many months: 'I sleep
with it and eat with it. I become obsessed and possessed'. He
then chose the music – Gunther Schuller's *Symphony for Brasses*
and studied it. Then he began the actual search for the movements:

> To a dancer, movements and gestures come easily, too
> easily, but the exactly right ones have to be searched for

[1] 'Composing a Dance' by José Limon, *Juilliard Review*, Winter 1955

patiently. One has to dig, literally, into one's bones and muscles for them.[1]

He described the first alarming encounter with his company of seven male dancers when he had to start working not with paint and canvas, nor with stone, but with people. 'The first rehearsal is a terrifying experience' –

> Slowly the work gathered momentum and before many rehearsals it seemed to dictate its own progression. This is one of the great mysteries of composition. A work has a way of taking hold and almost to compose itself. For awhile only, unfortunately, for suddenly one is faced with the bleak necessity to dig again, and reanimate, and to make a fresh start.[2]

Lucas Hoving who took the part of the leader, the Christ figure, has described how he waited and waited for his movements to be evolved; but always they were postponed. 'What for me; what for me?' Only late in the development was it possible for his difficult rôle to emerge.

Even though Limon worked from the basis of a character in a well-known story, he wrote:

> The important thing is, and should be, the movement. The idea is only the springboard, the pretext for a dance. The literary implications are, in the last analysis, secondary, and are used solely to colour movement and gesture. . . . It (dance) has always existed to give us that which nothing else can, certainly no other art. It has its own very special means of entering into the deeps of our awareness and there to move us ineffably.[3]

There are many teachers in schools who do not understand that time is needed for the imagination to work on an idea if it is to be pursued in depth; and there are many who feel the need of the support of a story, but who do not understand that 'the idea is only a springboard . . . the literary implications are, in the last resort, secondary'.

There are schools where the process is understood, where, for example, a study of Milton's *Paradise Lost*, and even a current

[1] ibid   [2] ibid   [3] ibid

debate on hanging, have moved the dancers deeply, where time has been taken for the ideas to develop, and where the dancers had sufficient resources in movement to evolve these ideas in dance form.

Technique

The dancer faces some of the problems of the instrumentalist – in order to perform he needs to master his instrument, but his instrument is himself. In the professional field there is a strong tradition that the daily class is a necessity, and that this class, if it is to be useful, must make severe demands upon the dancer.

Certainly dancers put themselves through processes which appear to the observer to be almost impossibly strenuous and exacting. There is a considerable amount of repetition of each 'exercise' or pattern of action, and certain exercises are regarded as basic to the building and shaping of the instrument and are always included. Some of these patterns are brief, and appear to be very narrow and limited rhythmically; others, especially with practised dancers, are longer, more complex and of the nature of brief dances.

If it is necessary (as indeed it must be) for muscles and joints to be exercised in demanding ways, and for the dancers to be dripping and exhausted at the end of a class, what is the impact of this process on them as persons and artists?

> One mustn't clamp down on energy. I think that's the worst thing about class, by its very nature it has a tendency to clamp down on it. In dance training one must open out so that one can be flexible. I don't mean to dismiss skill or anything like that, but flexibility is most important.
>
> I think that dance training must help you to be aware.[1]

Merce Cunningham is obviously aware that the sense of being alive, which all dancers cherish, may easily be destroyed by the cramping demands of a technique class which, by *mechanical* repetition, fails to develop the fundamental energy into real power.

[1] Merce Cunningham – interview

Another American dancer and teacher said:

I feel that technique is an expressive experience. I don't
feel there is such a thing as technique, I feel that it's all
human behaviour. If you point your foot, that is a sense of
energy, it makes a statement. I think that one of the
dangerous things in this process of working mechanically in
a class, working from habit, is that you aren't working as a
total person, being totally in the moment and totally aware
of the sensations of what your body is doing and what the
expressiveness of the particular thing you are doing
contains within it.

Somebody once said that technique is a way of doing a
thing. A technique has to service, has to really end up by
having trained you, servicing you. It has to really teach you
how to jump, and you have to jump enough so you *can*
jump, and you have to jump enough so that you've got the
energy to jump a long while.[1]

It is quite clear in this statement that there can be no escaping
persistence of practice if you are to become a professional dancer –
'You have to jump enough so that you've got the energy to jump
a long while.' But you need to jump as a *dancer*, not as an athlete –
'. . . aware of what the expressiveness of the particular thing you
are doing contains within it.'

In working merely mechanically, even though joints may be
mobilised and muscles strengthened, the dancer uses his body as
an object, and what he does is controlled, and indeed bound, by
the specific properties of that object – inert and stiff – and which
he must try to modify and extend. Mechanical practice is not an
expressive process but an impressive one – object (body) bound.
The inner, feeling impulse, is stillborn and does not, therefore,
illuminate the action. In dance practice which is expressive,
although there may be a strong element of routine, the feeling
impulse is the mainspring, irradiating the action which embodies
the feeling and reinforces it. Although the body as a limiting
object is still encountered, it no longer dominates.

Most of the dancers who have submitted to, but have been

[1] Jane Dudley – interview

illuminated by intensive practice, have expressed this experience very clearly:

> Each body movement is preceded by an inner movement . . . Expressive dance is just that – to move in harmony with the inner movement, and to have the inner movement brought out by the body movement. I try to explain to people that it goes both ways?[1]

And further:

> Proper dancing is affirmation. . . . It's the joy of existing. Therefore to sweat in training is something so marvellous. Who would go through it unless one really affirms this?[2]

If the need for contrast practice is admitted, as it certainly is by great professional dancers, it is clear that the mode of practice is crucial if the dancers are not to be merely athletic or, worse, dull. It is improbable that the dancer who practises mechanically, his body an object, can ever call up a deep response from an audience.

> I will say when I see an athlete do something awfully well, 'I would like to see it again', but it does not occur to me that I would like to do that particular movement, and I am not transported, I know I am looking *on*. When you looked at Pavlova you never thought 'I see this'; but 'I *feel* it; I dance myself'. And when I saw Isadora dancing I had no *thoughts*, I had the happiness of dancing.[3]

Dancers who are also choreographers are able to balance and blend the technical needs of their dancers with the process of creating compositions in a way that many teachers of classes are not in a position to do. Technique can so easily be separated from the creative process.

> With the Company sometimes in class I work at a little bit (of a projected composition) to see how it looks. And then I make it into exercises, and sometimes I can see further into it.[4]

Cunningham conducted a Workshop experiment for a month

[1] Kurt Jooss – interview
[2] ibid
[3] Marie Rambert – interview
[4] Merce Cunningham – interview

with thirty-five young people to help them understand how a dance was made.

> They not only got to do a dance but they got to see what the working procedure is, that you have to do something clearly but within that you also have freedoms. You do everything with a great deal of respect for the other person, but you have to be very strict in what you do. You have to be clear and sharp about what you do, with this awareness of the other person. And you can only find this out through a working atmosphere. What I am getting at really here is to say that a way must be found to point out to anybody that they must be disciplined from *within*, not from something out here. I don't like that. But if the person understands the necessity for something *within* himself then everything works out. There must, of course, be a certain degree of good faith.[1]

And Jooss, speaking of the evolution of *The Green Table* with his own company: 'I had very good dancers who were well able to improvise and many of the movements came from improvisation and discussion'. Choreography was a shared process between the company and the choreographer, who was also their teacher.

A similar experience came from working in Martha Graham's company:

> There is a way of watching movement which we call empathy, where you sense it through your own body, and that's the way to catch what a teacher is giving you. And if you can do that it's the most important thing. For example, for the choreographer. When we were working with Graham and she would start on a new piece, this sense of the level, the character, the atmosphere that she was working within, if you captured it you didn't have to be told where to put your arms. There developed this kind of rapport between a company and the choreographer, so that you are feeding the choreographer as much as she is feeding you. When this is arrived at it is an absolutely marvellous state.[2]

[1] Merce Cunningham – interview   [2] Jane Dudley – interview

Although this account springs from the fiercely demanding processes which are typical of the professional field, it might well be a description of the best sort of teaching in education, and not only in dance. The kind of continuity of experience and the reciprocity which enables both teacher and class to catch on to each other's feelings and intentions, and for each to feed the other, is the kind of situation which is not uncommon in English primary schools, a situation from which springs so much remarkable painting, writing, dancing and drama, and which can develop a generally sensitive level of perception.

The specialist teacher in a secondary school, who perhaps meets a class once or twice a week, finds it far more difficult. This is partly because the gaps in experience are too great (a class may dance only once a week), and partly because it is nearly impossible to establish the sort of relationship that is much easier to achieve in the working atmosphere to which Merce Cunningham refers, and which can happen easily in a primary school.

Again Jane Dudley, formerly a notable member of Martha Graham's company, and now a teacher, is illuminating about the nature of teaching:

> You've got to work with the deep inside of a person, and that's what teaching is – you change a person, and this is hard to do because the person has resistances, and doesn't want to be tampered with, and has all sorts of defences, and this is where a teacher has to confront, and be willing to dredge it out of the teacher's self, in order to dredge it out of the other person, and this is what I call teaching, and I think a lot of what is being done is a total negation of this, of getting at the interior. A lot of what happens is just kooky.[1]

CHILDREN

Teachers of children, especially in schools, where the somewhat ruthless pressures of the professional field do not obtain, but where humane considerations predominate, have to face the continuing problem of how to meet the needs of the apparently

[1] Jane Dudley – interview

inept as well as of the naturally gifted. In education 'technique' is often regarded as a dirty word implying something that has a deadening effect, the purpose of which is not always apparent. Perhaps 'practice' is more easily understood as necessary and therefore acceptable, and avoids the connotations that have grown up round the term technique.

But in dance, of what kinds may this practice be? At one end are the strictly patterned actions which the class is expected to repeat as exactly as possible. They must endeavour to copy not only *what* is done but *how* it is done, following the timing precisely. At the other end an exact pattern is not set, but the *quality* of action is demanded – for example, to move with sustained slowness or brilliant speed, to move with strong or with light tension, to extend experience in space, or to focus on and awaken different parts of the body.

At the one end there is the risk that the teacher and the class may become bound by a process which consists of a series of recipes (well tried and providing a sense of security) and involvement in depth may be lost. At the other, where the emphasis is on quality, and the pattern of movement is not specified, involvement is more readily achieved, but the framework is so wide that the teacher may fail to be sufficiently explicit, so that the children do not reach far enough beyond their natural habits of movement. In adolescence, especially, they may well withdraw because they do not command an adequate form in which the inner impulse can be embodied, recognised and strengthened.

The object of teaching at all stages is to help the learner to develop his resources so that these are adequate for achieving the ends he wants to pursue.[1]

EARLY STAGES

In the early stages, both before and on entry to school, it is important to preserve and enhance the openness and exuberance in action which is natural to young children and which, even at five years, may have been quenched by lack of space, by a parent's sense of propriety, as well as by adult exasperation which,

[1] This problem is explored very lucidly by A. N. Whitehead in two lectures: 'The Rhythm of Education' and 'The Rhythmic Claims of Freedom and Discipline' published in *The Aims of Education*, Benn

understandably but sometimes too often, leads to the command to 'shut up'.

Young children certainly practise – crawling, walking, rolling, climbing and manipulating. They learn much through the sense of touch, by no means restricted to the hands, but by the pressure of different parts of the body on various surfaces, and through these processes they experience and manage the weight of their bodies.

> Playing with gravity and defeating it – children do it the whole time. I have noticed two significant moments with my own children. One is that they dare to jump, and this happens between two and three years – jumping on the spot, able to go up half-an-inch, to *dare* to leave the ground. Then it turns into jumping off stairs, higher and higher, so that it gets more terrifying.
>
> I worked in Sam's (my youngest) playgroup and I always used to go with mattresses, and there was a table, and they would jump off the table on to these mats for 45 minutes, landing in every conceivable way and, in the air, jumping into different shapes, turning and landing backwards and so on. It was as if they could never get to the end of all the kinds of jumping that there were. They couldn't get enough of it. At the end of two years (when they were rising five) they had such mastery of their bodies; when new children arrived at that stage, and joined in the jumping, the difference was extraordinary.[1]

One can only surmise the processes that these children may have gone through. Clearly, since they would continue for 45 minutes on end, and for two years, jumping fulfilled a deep need. In this repetition of the act of jumping they were certainly practising the management of themselves in the air, but the process was also an exploratory and inventive one – 'It was as if they could never get to the end of all the kinds of jumping that there were.' It seems likely that sometimes the body was more of an object to be manipulated, and that sometimes the feeling-impulse, 'Here am I, in the air', would be the dominating experience, and the action predominantly expressive, recalling the inner sense experience.

[1] Veronica Sherborne – interview

Play, which has such a flexible connotation, and which covers exploration, practice and invention, and which may be mundane in intention or primarily expressive, is perhaps the appropriate word.

ATHLETIC OR EXPRESSIVE

A boy playing with a ball can be seen to be intent on the control of that object, kicking it, bouncing it, throwing it, hitting it – adjusting his actions to its size, weight and degree of resilience. He is akin to the athlete. The same boy leaping impulsively with excitement or, perhaps, sitting and swaying as he hums to himself, is impelled by and involved with the inner disturbance which lights up, is reinforced by and recognised through the expressive medium – in this instance, movement. He is akin to the dancer.

A child has need of each mode – that of the athlete and that of the dancer – and the adult needs to recognise both.

PRIMARY SCHOOL

We (children especially) are moved, literally, by feeling, but as school becomes more sedentary (as it tends to from about the age of seven), and success in the use of language predominates, movement as a means of understanding feeling is damped down and crippled. This is not to decry the extraordinary value of language, but to insist on the need for the use of other media, and especially of movement where the person is both instrument and medium.

> The expression of emotion is not, as it were, a dress made to fit an emotion already existing, but it is an activity without which the experience of that emotion cannot exist. Take away the language, and you take away what is expressed; there is nothing left but crude feeling at the merely psychic level. . . .
>
> There is no way of expressing the same feeling in two different media. This is true both of the relation between different systems of speech, and of the relation between vocal language and other forms of language. . . . Music is one order of languages and speech is another; each expresses what

it does express with absolute clarity and precision; but what they express is two different types of emotion, each proper to itself. The same is true of manual gesture. . . .

Now, if a person acquires the ability to express one kind of emotion and not another, the result will be that he knows the one kind to be in him, but not the other. Those others will be in him as mere brute feelings, never mastered and controlled, but either concealed in the darkness of his own self-ignorance or breaking in upon him in the shape of passion storms, which he can neither control nor understand. Consequently, if a civilization loses all power of expression except through the voice, and then asserts that the voice is the best expressive medium, it is simply saying that it knows of nothing in itself that is worth expressing except what can be thus expressed; and that is a tautology, for it merely means 'what we (members of this particular society) do not know we do not know', except so far as it suggests the addition: 'and we do not wish to find out'.[1]

The boy referred to on page 19 of the present book, is a prime example of one who discovered in dance movement a means of coming to terms with his violent behaviour 'breaking in upon him in the shape of passion storms which he can neither control nor understand'.

THE NEED FOR SPACE AND TIME

Space and time are needed for movement if the natural ability and openness of the children is not to be damped down and their perception blunted. Space, which is expensive, is grudged by those who have to handle building costs, and time is often grudged by teachers who do not realise that movement is a prime need if children are to be fully alive. Yet in schools where movement plays a full part the children are not merely lively, but are perceptive generally. Such statements cannot be proved experimentally, because there are so many dimensions to the school situation. The impact of one kind of experience cannot be isolated, but observation of the general nature of children at this stage suggests that too sedentary a programme is likely to be deadening or to lead to outbursts.

[1] *The Principles of Art* by R. G. Collingwood, Oxford University Press

SOME ELEMENTS IN TEACHING

The most important element in teaching is the quality of the relationship that is developed between the teacher and the class. All adults remember those teachers who made learning most easily possible; nearly always they are those for whom they had affection.

A relationship which is established in the classroom, where the transition from one medium to another is easy and natural, and where individual contact can be made without difficulty, seems too often to be disturbed when the class moves into the hall. Partly the move (which usually has to be timetabled) may have been untimely, partly the exuberant action which a space is likely to trigger off and which must first be satisfied, makes it difficult to re-establish the degree of absorption current in the classroom; but, most of all, the teacher seems to become a different person, abandoning the manner and mode of teaching which he practises elsewhere. His relationship is no longer that of person to person, but of teacher to class, and he expects a class response. He may even blow a whistle (appropriate for football) or bang a drum in order to attract attention. The larger space is not entirely responsible, and there are teachers who work in the hall as quietly and intimately as they do in the classroom.

Every word spoken by the teacher, every gesture, every stillness creates a framework within which the children can, or cannot, function. Words, especially the sound of words, must be used to evoke action, and children are remarkably quick in picking up cues from tone of voice and gesture. 'Give it a right good wuff,' (in a broad Yorkshire accent) unlocked tremendous energy in the effort to throw balls very high, and 'Get up slowly, slowly; feel it from the inside,' spoken with the teacher's own inner feeling for the quality of movement, made it possible for each child to begin to discover and deeply involve himself in his own quality of slowness.

At the primary stage children move very readily from one mode of movement to another – from the acrobatic or athletic to dance or dance-like movement, or to a mode the flavour of which is predominantly that of drama. This can happen quite naturally, but the emphasis is also dependent upon the kind of resources the children are helped to develop – athletic, or expressive, or both. A teacher needs to be able to discern the mode in which the children are working, whether they are working objectively as in the kind of activity that is often labelled 'agility', or expressively. A hand-spring or a cartwheel may be no more than a skilful acrobatic feat, but it may also be used as an expression of exuberance flung into the rhythm of a dance. It is not that one mode is 'better' than the other, but that the usage is different.

A teacher needs to be able to discern whether, for example, a child who is supposedly dancing is merely going through the motions (as may easily happen when precisely taught steps and straight lines are emphasised). The fact that music is being played at the same time is no guarantee that a child is really involved. He needs to note whether a boy moving across the room is merely walking from one point to another, or whether he is deeply involved in the feeling of his walking, or in the process of becoming some character.

There are so many children scattered over the space, so many different elements in their work in a medium which leaves no trace to be examined at leisure, as writing or a painting can be, that a teacher's powers of observation are very considerably taxed. It is not merely seeing *what* happens, but also discerning what it means – for example, the boy's traverse of the room.

A primary teacher knows the children in so many different contexts, and their work in so many media, that this is less difficult than at first appears. But it is on the basis of this discernment that the development of the children's experience must be based.

If particular resources seem to need to be developed – for example, focus on a more flexible use of certain parts of the body, a greater understanding of firmness and stability, or awareness of certain elements of space – then the terms of reference will be set fairly closely in order to help the children to become more alive to certain qualities of movement. The broader the terms of reference – perhaps the choice of a certain tune, or pattern of sounds, or pattern of encounters, the wider the freedom to choose, and the more the children need their own time (not measured in minutes) to work in. The gradual widening of the terms of reference means that the area of choice grows naturally and imperceptibly, balanced and fed by the more 'technical' process of building up resources in movement. No hard and fast line need appear, it is as if a tide, or current, flowed from teacher to children and again to the teacher, the to and fro being sometimes in rapid succession, and sometimes flowing strongly, and for a longer period, in one direction or the other.

When music is played it can be an indication of whether the children have the resources to respond with discrimination, aware, without analysis, of phrasing and dynamic quality, or whether they can only manage a general and superficial response.

In one class which had developed very rich resources, a visitor tried the experiment of playing a record of a Mozart minuet. The children listened to it twice and then got up and moved to it and, as the visitor (who was a very knowledgeable one) said: 'Suddenly the room was full of courtiers'. The same class could respond with gusto to a folk tune, jazz or Spanish music, and with an astonishing command of phrasing.

Such discrimination is not so much taught, as that term is usually understood, but rather made possible by the teacher, who has created opportunities for the children to develop rich resources in action involving not only versatility and skill but also the nourishment of the inner feeling response. The music is not analysed, they *know* its essential quality in their bones.

THE NEXT STAGE

The end of the primary stage – the stage of openness, eagerness and resilience – does not, of course, coincide with the move to the secondary phase of education which, in England, still takes place most usually at about eleven years. In many such schools the characteristics of children at the primary stage are found to persist for at least a year (indeed there may appear to be a certain reversion to childishness) and begin to fade thereafter; but in one secondary school where the children enter at thirteen from the surrounding middle schools, the very observant headmaster remarked that the children showed most of the characteristics of eleven year old entrants, with the exception of the girls in the field of dance where they appeared awkward and self-conscious. How far the persistence of primary characteristics is dependent upon status in a school – being the youngest perhaps prolongs the stage and postpones adolescence – and how far this depends upon a fundamental stage of development is difficult to say, but at thirteen many, but not all, girls are clearly adolescent, while many but not all, boys, still have the characteristics of 'little' boys.

But in English schools the drastic change is, perhaps, that instead of close contact with one teacher, and the easy transition from one medium to another, the children encounter a number of different 'specialist' teachers who may, or may not, build a sense of security because of their expertise in their subject, but who certainly do not have the opportunity of establishing the kind of relationship with the children that makes for situations in which the 'miraculous' can occur. The change to a number of teachers, the movement to different specialist rooms may, of course, be stimulating, especially at first, but there is nothing stimulating about the parcelling of the day into thirtyfive- or forty-minute periods for most subjects.

Dance, where it exists, is usually under the aegis of physical education instead of being, much more suitably, linked with other arts, especially drama. One consequence is that it shares the time available for P.E. with gymnastics, games, swimming and so on, and is usually allocated one period a week of 35 to 40 minutes (the net time is some 25–30 minutes). The situation is an impossible one. Dance is a medium in which the children are easily led to feel exposed, and they need the confidence given by a teacher who is not only knowledgeable, but who knows them and is known by them, so as to found that mutual trust on which the practice of any art so much depends.

In thirty minutes or so an attempt must be made to build up a transition between the sedentary mode of the classroom and that of expressive action, to develop resources in movement, and to give time for the imagination to get to work. If, by some happy chance, the occasion lights up, it is over too soon, and there is then a yawning gap of a week (filled of course with other subject lessons) between that occasion and the next one. No roots are struck from which further growth can take place, and after about a couple of years the realisation of ineptness is translated into the condemnation, 'It's kid's stuff', and indeed, too often, it is. A few naturally gifted children may not feel at a loss.

There are schools where the use of time is understood, where those elements that need comparatively brief and frequent periods of practice (such as the early stages of a foreign language, or the beginning of swimming) are balanced by those which need a span of time. Double periods are usually allocated to art and to football. To art because materials have to be brought out, arranged and put away, rather than because the whole mode of working needs time for medium and impulse to play upon each other. To football because it takes time for boys to change, get on to the field, play, and have a shower.

In these schools where the nature of the subjects is understood, the use of time is adjusted accordingly so that a quarter, a half or a whole day may be allocated, together with brief periods where these are needed.

But, within the phases of measured time, there occur those crucial, personal experiences of unmeasured time in which the creative process takes place. In her film *A Dancer's World*, Martha Graham refers to 'the pressure of time' in the ten years that it takes to make a dancer. Whenever the element of practice is in the forefront of experience it seems to take place against the pressure of time, but the creative process (in whatever medium) is experienced in timelessness, a phase that may be very brief or prolonged, and may even be manifested by apparent inactivity. Within a system of specialist teaching, with time rigidly measured, it is difficult to create opportunities in which timelessness may be experienced (such phases cannot of course be ordained) or to recognise such experiences when they occur.

DEVELOPMENTS

As children change gradually into young women and young men the earlier effervescence, with all its charm, disappears, to be replaced by considerably extended powers, more passionate feelings and a deep need for self-realisation. The problem is how to enhance the individual's awareness of himself by so developing his resources in the medium that the deep impulse of feeling is not quenched or constrained, but is strengthened, controlled and enjoyed without self-indulgence or fear.

There are groups, and there are individuals, who indulge in the feeling impulse and in whom the lack of form leads to the manifestation of mere symptoms of feeling. At the other extreme are groups where patterns of action are strictly taught and practised to the exclusion of other experience. Either of these extremes imposes limitations. In one the impulse runs riot, in the other the medium may imprison. The concentration on set patterns may stem from the need to feel safe, both on the part of the teacher and of the group, and may all too easily degenerate into mechanical action, though no great professional dancer would have it so. 'One of the dangerous things in this process of working mechanically in class, working from habit, is that you are not working as a total person, totally in the moment, and totally aware of the sensations of what your body is doing, and what the expressiveness of the particular thing you are doing contains within it'.[1]

Finding the means whereby the inner impulse is understood and strengthened through the medium of movement is a continuing process varying for each person and each group at different stages. On the one hand there may be, at times, a need to emphasise the management of oneself as an object – 'You have to jump enough so that you've got the energy to jump a long time',[2] on the other the need to stimulate the inner disturbance which energises action.

'Expressive dance is just that – to move in harmony with the inner movement, and to have the inner movement brought out by the body movement'.[3] It is in this process that the inner impulse is recalled and recognised, recall and recognition being crucial to the development and understanding of oneself. A teacher describes this in relation to her own pupils:

> It's something they can recapture; it's something that's alive. If they're finding, through a particular thing they've created, that it helps them to discover themselves, they can recapture the experience again.[4]

[1] Jane Dudley – interview
[2] ibid (see page 43)
[3] Kurt Jooss – interview
[4] Sue Morris – interview

A dancer may be stirred by many different stimuli – by movement itself, by a piece of music (Bach, the Beatles, a Negro spiritual), by ideas such as 'Touch', 'Growth', 'Time', 'Argument'. Sometimes they are lit up by a poem, a painting or a piece of sculpture.

Development does not rest on the 'subject' chosen, but in the way in which the dancer responds to it and develops it – not literally, but symbolically, in the medium of dance – showing increasingly complex levels of the experience of feeling.

A young coloured dancer who chose as her springboard the spiritual *Steal Away to Jesus* might well have been swamped by the feeling impulse roused by the music and by the sentiment of the piece. But she was able, with clarity and with simplicity, to transmute the spiritual into forms of action which articulated for her (and indeed for those who watched her) her deeply felt understanding of what the piece stood for. There was no hint of imitative action, or of literal meaning; even such gestures which were recognisable as related to those of prayer, praise, and submission were intensive realisations in symbolic form of the deep experience of these states.

In group compositions the dancer must not only be able to realise his own inner impulse of feeling by his own actions, but also incorporate the expressive actions of others, otherwise there is no real response, but a mere experience of close proximity, involving some agreement as to direction, shape and tempo, but nothing of greater potency. As dancers become more assured in respect of their own development they are able to expand this by entering into, and sharing, the experience of others.

At this stage (in England designated as secondary), young men and women should be able so to strengthen their experience of the relationship between the inner impulse and its expression in action that they may neither be torn by emotion, nor sullen because the inner impulse has been deadened, nor suffer acute self-consciousness because their means of expression in the medium are inadequate.

Boys are seldom given the experience of dance; it is held to be effeminate, though often more strenuous than most sports and games. It is understandable within the current English tradition that boys are afraid that their sense of manhood may be assailed, especially, as so often happens, if the prospective teacher is a woman. Their vulnerability has to be understood and respected, yet the stories of their destructiveness suggest that sport is not enough to enable them to come to terms with themselves. Certainly when they are given suitable opportunities to dance their response is tremendous and it appears that there is a hunger that needs to be satisfied.

Jooss refers to dancing as 'affirmation'.

Douglas Kennedy as 'the sense that it gives you of being alive in a living world'.

Such experiences should assuredly belong to being young.

Ye who dance not know not what we are knowing

This quotation from the Apocryphal *Hymn of Jesus* asserts the unique mode of knowing which belongs to dance. Collingwood emphasises that 'there is no way of expressing the same feeling in two different media', and that 'if a person acquires the ability to express one kind of emotion and not another, the result will be that he knows the one kind to be in him, but not the other. These others will be in him as mere brute feelings'.[1]

What is known by the dancer? 'Knowledge of many feelings',[2] but such knowledge is common to expressive experience in any medium, though peculiar to each. 'Dance creates a world of powers, made visible by the unbroken fabric of gesture. That is what makes dance a different art from the others'.[3]

'A world of powers' – from time immemorial, dance was a means of invoking the Powers that Be; it is no longer so used in Western civilisation, except in isolated pockets. But the dancer, who is himself both instrument and medium, is intimately aware, in the very fabric of his being, of the powers he creates in the process of releasing the impulse which generates energy in dynamic form and which reciprocates and regenerates the impulse. It is this that the dancer knows. He is above himself.

[1] *The Principles of Art* by R. G. Collingwood, Oxford University Press
[2] *Problems of Art* by Susanne K. Langer, Routledge & Kegan Paul   [3] ibid

Dance and music

In most people's minds dance is irrevocably associated with music, but many musicians would prefer not to connect music with dance, certainly not 'great' music written without that intent in the mind of the composer.

The music that has been associated with dance ranges from that of the bells worn by dancers, drums and clappers, pipe and tabor (all in the folk tradition), to the minuets of Mozart (certainly written to be danced to), symphonies by Tschaikowsky and Brahms (used by Massine), Franck's *Symphonic Variations* (used by Ashton), Bach's *Passacaglia* and *Fugue in C Minor* (used by Doris Humphreys) and, recently, a late Beethoven quartet (used by Paul Taylor for his composition *Orbs*). Music specially composed includes the dances in Purcell's opera *Dido and Aeneas*, in Gluck's *Orpheus*, Tschaikowsky's *Sleeping Beauty* and *Swan Lake*, Stravinsky's *Petrouchka*, Vaughan Williams' *Job*, Bernstein's *West Side Story*. The classic collaboration was between Fokine, Stravinsky and Benois in *Petrouchka*; in our own time, the prime example is that of Cunningham and Cage with Rauschenberg as designer. A notable element in this last collaboration was the fact that all three were actually present at performances, and permitted themselves considerable flexibility so that no two performances were alike, though the changes were within well understood terms of reference.

Cunningham has stated that 'it is hard for many people to accept that dancing has nothing in common with music other than the element of time and division of time'.[1] In one of his compositions, *Variations V*, John Cage was commissioned to prepare a score and 'John decided to find out if there might not be ways that the sound could be affected by movement and he and David Tudor proceeded to find out what these were.' The final solution was '. . . a series of poles, twelve in all, like antennae, placed over the stage, each to have a sound radius, sphere shaped, of four feet. When a dancer came into this radius sound would result. Each antenna was to have a different sound and some had several'. To these were added a series of photo-electric cells. The movements of the dancers triggered off the sounds, 'but the kind

[1] *Changes – Notes on Choreography* by Merce Cunningham, Something Else Press, New York

of sound, how long it might be, or the possible repetition of it was controlled by the musicians who were at the various machines behind us'.[1]

This seems a far cry from the intimate association between an Indian dancer and the accompanying group of musicians, where the communion is so close that accompaniment hardly seems to be the right word, it is as if music and dance were one and the same growth, and it is unthinkable that they should be evolved separately.

The most obvious element in the association of dance and music is that of movement arising from excitement. Movement is the source of sound whether produced vocally or by the stamping of feet or clapping of hands, and both music and dance emerge when people are excited, exalted, indeed when they celebrate. It is often held that dance and instrumental music developed together, rather than dancing and singing. Yet, as in dancing so in singing, the person is both instrument and medium and the personal involvement is similar, perhaps deeper. Primitive people, and many folk groups, sing *as* they dance. For example, 'mouth music' often accompanies Hebridean dances.

> If you see the Zulus when they dance, although they have drums and clappers, they don't necessarily use these, not even at the start; but what they always do is this chant. And the sound that comes out is as much an expression of the body as the movement itself, and if you didn't see the movement and hear the chant you could visualize the movement without having seen it; it's so in keeping. Similarly if you couldn't hear the sound and you could see the movement (as you might on television) you would know the sounds by just watching the movements. It comes from the same place.[2]

The relationship between action and music seems obvious to one young musician who has accompanied dancers, composed for their choreography and also for their singing:

> For me music is more and more an extension of the bodily functions, rather than simply a technical craft. If you're

[1] *Changes – Notes on Choreography* by Merce Cunningham, Something Else Press, New York   [2] Douglas Kennedy – interview

playing the clarinet you must become something that moves. I wonder sometimes whether people realize fully the impetus in a piece of music. Sometimes when I listen to a chord, if I am standing up I literally fall forward.

More and more I am interested in the voice, less and less interested in instruments. I presume that is because the voice is the first instrument we have, and it is so wrapped up with the body.[1]

He continued:

Basically it's the same thing that makes us dance that makes us sing. I think this is why, at present, I am so interested in writing for the voice, because it's nearest to us. It is *us*.

The term rhythm would seem, quite properly, to be shared by both music and dance, though it is also used in connection with, for example, architecture and painting. It stands for a number of different things to different people, the most limited and in-accurate being, perhaps, what they usually mean by 'a rhythm', i.e. a short pattern of sounds; this is often further restricted to the pattern of sounds between bar lines and to time signatures, e.g. 3/4, 6/8. While these elements are not irrelevant they are in-sufficient, since rhythm is much more closely related to phrases than to bars, which can become a barrier to rhythmic performance.

The essence of rhythm is the preparation of a new event by the ending of a previous one. A person who moves rhythmi-ally need not repeat a single motion exactly. His movements, however, must be complete gestures, so that one can sense a beginning, intent, and consummation, and see in the last stage of one the condition and indeed the rise of another.[2]

Illustrated in a simple form – we breathe in, to breathe out, to breathe in. A player lifts his tennis racquet in preparation (musically speaking the anacrusis) for the stroke which is its consequence. If he is skilled, and his opponent has not hurried him off his stroke, one phase follows the other inevitably. But when an inept player lifts his racquet in preparation it at once becomes evident that, as it were, there is no future in it.

[1] Gordon Jones – interview
[2] *Feeling and Form* by Susanne K. Langer, Routledge & Kegan Paul

'Everything that prepares a future creates rhythm'.[1] The upbeat of the conductor, the dissonance before its resolution, the pause (in music or in dance) which, like the holding of breath, presages the impetus which follows.

Douglas Kennedy describes the relationship of music and movement in some of the Yugoslav Horas, the chain dances that go on and on:

> They will take a long piece of music and do it to a succession of shorter pieces of dance, or vice versa, a long, long dance that has several miles of straight line before it changes and do that to short lengths of music. What happens when you do that is an association for a time of relationship, pulsations going on and on, and then comes a moment when the music comes to an end and the dance goes on, and then the music comes in again, and the arm-in-arm is not quite the same, and they are not quite linked. And then comes a point where by virtue of the several lengths coming together again by pure coincidence, there is an astonishing sense of renewed meeting which is so exciting that the thing has a new burst of energy.
>
> I think it's very important to realise this feature because it makes you understand why the relationship of music to dance when it's purely mathematical is only interesting mathematically. To a dancer this isn't important. But when you get this disassociation of mathematical precision, and after a time there is coincidence again, it's like an atomic bomb, and that is what you notice in Balkan dancing – that every now and then they get a complete renewal of life, as if another charge had been added.[2]

Speaking of the problems of accompanying a dance class Gordon Jones says: 'If an exercise is being counted out – one, two, three, then one is not playing in rhythm if one just plays one, two, three, because there is no moment when it takes off. It's like the breath before the thing, and until that's implied, or actually there, it's dead'.[3]

Increasingly instruments other than the piano, for example drums, are used to accompany classes, or to provide the music

1 *Feeling and Form* by Susanne K. Langer, Routledge & Kegan Paul
2 Douglas Kennedy – interview   3 Gordon Jones – interview

for choreography. Less and less are dancers submerged in a thick texture and big volume of sound; rather is a real partnership set up between, for example, two dancers and a flute with plucked strings, or between a singer and a dancer. Where Indian music, with its tradition of improvisation, is practised, a fine and sensitive element in the dance seems to emerge. In schools the advent of Orff-type instruments makes it easily possible for the dancers themselves to provide the music instead of relying on records or tapes, often of a heavily orchestrated kind.

It would be a limitation if all composed music were to be omitted. For one thing it may well prevent dancers from listening to music they might otherwise miss; for another, if the dancers have sufficient resources to bring to the composition, their contact with music can greatly expand their experience.

Perhaps if one word were chosen to represent what the dancer may seek and gain from the music it is impetus – impetus that belongs to a Bach chorale, to a folk song or to improvisation on a group of drums.

Like the children (described on page 53) whose response to a Mozart minuet was so discriminating, the dancer may bring to music a response which, while it is not analytical, is certainly not unmusical, and may well be more rhythmical than some musicians might appreciate.

Drama

Anyone can act?

If the producer of a play were to encounter an acquaintance and ask him to act in his production there is a fair chance that after discussion, and despite lack of training or experience, the invitation would be accepted. A similar invitation to play the violin, or to dance before an audience without previous training or experience, would be refused. There is an assumption that acting is 'natural' – an extension of ordinary experiences, using the coinage of everyday gesture and speech, heightened by lighting, costume, make-up and an audience.

All over the country there is a multitude of amateur dramatic societies giving public performances to their admiring friends, and sometimes to wider and more critical audiences. There are also schools which, without any other experience of drama, indulge in the annual ritual of the School Play, although they would be unlikely to play football matches unless that game was included in the school programme.

It is certainly true that the 'natural actor' exists, and this is perhaps the source of much disagreement as to how professional actors should be trained – in a Drama School, or through a gradual extension of experience in the theatre. No such argument exists in connection with dancers; trained, it is agreed, they must be, and the training continues even when they have achieved high professional status. There is even a considerable measure of agreement, where Classical Ballet is concerned, as to the ingredients of that training. But:

With acting anyone *can* do it up to a point. There is
amateur acting, there is good amateur acting, and there are
lots of amateurs who have become professionals; it's the
process through which they go that counts. The energy
which the individual actor produces in his work, he has to
learn from that work, and to learn from the people he
works with. I don't say it's necessarily wrong to have
drama schools, but I don't think there is a simple answer to
that question as there is in the dance world.[1]

In the autumn of 1973 there was a startling performance in the
London theatre by two actors who performed as professionals
for the first time. One critic described them as 'acting with an
intensity and flair that is beyond words, they gave us a performance of rare brilliance.' These were two black South African
actors with no training other than the experience gained in
acting in missionary, High School and amateur group productions. It may be that such achievement emerged partly because
their improvised play *Sizwe Bansi is Dead* manifested experiences
that stirred them to the depths, partly because there seems to be
less of a block than there is in the white races between the inner
impulse and its expression in action.

The impulse to dance stems from the experience of being
above oneself, but the impulse to act emerges from the need to
explore other identities and other situations. A young child
becomes his father, the doctor, the teacher, the Red Indian. He
climbs a height or swings on a rope, and is at once a more
generalised high-up or swinging creature. A shawl, funny hat,
boots, a long skirt, trigger off a number of changes.

We enjoy acts of impersonation and even practise them in
everyday life. We play the part of a good mother, an obedient
daughter or a rebellious son (who, later, may become a stern
father), and the parts we play alter according to our relationship
with others, so that the good mother can also be an impatient
daughter, the obedient daughter a mean sister, the rebellious son
a humble lover. We are also capable of 'putting on an act', and
we recognise this behaviour in others; it stands, usually, for
behaviour that is, quite consciously, superficial, and is confused by
some amateurs with the art of acting.

[1] William Gaskill – interview

The professional theatre

THE NATURE OF ACTING

There is much in the training and experience of professional actors that is relevant to personal development and to communication in everyday life. First of all is the actor's exploration of himself:

> The actor has himself as his field of work. This field is richer than that of the painter, richer than that of the musician, because to explore he needs to call on every aspect of himself. His hand, his eye, his ear and his heart are what he is studying with. Seen this way, acting is a life's work – the actor is step by step extending his knowledge of himself through the painful, ever-changing circumstances of rehearsal and the tremendous punctuation points of performance.[1]

This point of view is echoed by a young actor, Neil Johnston, 'It's a search for oneself, not an indulgence of oneself. One's growth both as a person and as an actor is immeasurable'.[2]

In the course of this exploration in which 'the actor has himself as his field of work' the wholeness of experience begins to be apprehended, and the actor realises that thinking and feeling, and physical and mental, are not separate processes.

> I do believe that the theatre is the only place where you actually reconcile the physical and the mental, the pagan and the spiritual, the intellectual and emotional, or whatever divisions are foisted upon us. Where you actually see people behaving as a whole, and this is very, very important.[3]

Jane Howell, at that time Director of the Northcott Theatre, went on to recall part of her experience as a university student:

> I understood it in my head (and I have been very lucky in my teachers), but it's taken me ten years to understand it in my body. It's not until you meet that situation yourself that you find you can understand anything.[4]

[1] *The Empty Space* by Peter Brook, MacGibbon & Kee
[2] Neil Johnston – interview   [3] Jane Howell – interview   [4] ibid

While there is an emphasis on an actor's exploration of himself this process cannot be self-centred or self-indulgent; it does not take place in a vacuum, but in the company of other actors who act and re-act on each other and so push forward, or in unfortunate circumstances hinder, the process of discovery. It is a situation that demands generosity and gentleness, and while the group needs to work as a group each member must also be able to work as an individual.

An example of the process of discovery made by one actor in the course of working with another was described by Neil Johnston.[1] In the course of evolving the fight, under water, between Beowulf and the water witch, Grendel's mother, each in confronting the other found that they were also confronting something in themselves. 'I was fascinated in finding the female principle in myself – a feeling in one's bones. I can intellectualise on this, but whether I can *sense* it in me, and feel it in me, is completely different.'

Awareness of each other leads to the sensitive interplay which is fundamental to the art of acting.

> Contact is one of the most essential things. Often when an actor speaks of contact, or thinks of contact, he believes that it means to gaze fixedly. But this is not contact. It is only a position, a situation. Contact is not staring, it is to see. Now I am in contact with you. I see which of you is against me. I see one person who is indifferent, another who listens with some interest, and someone who smiles. All this changes my actions; it is contact, and it forces me to change my way of acting.[2]

Grotowski continued in this speech to comment on the minute changes that occur within a rehearsed pattern, and the need for response to these minute changes. He illustrated this by the example of the variations in a neighbour's customary 'good morning'.

> The action and the intonation are the same, but the change in contact is so minute that it is impossible to analyze it rationally. This changes all relationships, and it is also the secret of harmony between men.[3]

[1] Neil Johnston – interview
[2] *Towards a Poor Theatre* by Jerzy Grotowski, Methuen   [3] ibid

Similarly, William Gaskill, in an interview:

> I seem to work on the principle that what one character
> says must have an effect on the other, and that between
> one person speaking something must happen which makes
> the other person alter.

And Peter Brook refers to:

> . . . the true unspectacular intimacy that long work and true
> confidence in other people brings about – on Broadway, a
> crude gesture of self-exposure is easy to come by, but this
> has nothing to do with the subtle, sensitive inter-relation
> between people working confidently together. When the
> Americans envy the British, it is this odd sensibility, this
> uneven give and take that they mean.[1]

This subtle awareness of others, leading to sensitive communication, is in the forefront of the demands made upon actors. Jane
Howell, discussing the purpose of the Japanese defensive and
martial arts practised by members of the company, said: 'It
seems to me that the thought of the mind was the movement of
the hand, and vice versa. They lead to one becoming aware of
the instinctive moment for action, which is dictated neither by
the body or the mind'.[2] She also referred to the time taken to
'create awareness of other people without competitiveness'.

The explorations of the actor are not only pursued in contact
with other actors, but are finally developed before an audience.
The actor lives out in public much that we might prefer to keep
hidden, not only from others, but from ourselves.

> He is actually being asked to expose himself, and taking
> your clothes off on the stage is nothing compared with what
> the good actor does all the time without taking his clothes
> off. He puts himself at risk. He's working with his emotions,
> and in a sense he is being paid to do that out there on
> behalf of us all. To go back to the Greek idea of the
> actors being priests – the priest is there, going further for
> the sake of everybody. That to me is where the serious
> side of the theatre should work. The actor is actually

[1] *The Empty Space* by Peter Brook, MacGibbon & Kee
[2] Jane Howell – interview

revealing parts of us to ourselves. He is doing it in public, and he should be striking sub-conscious chords in us all the time. These sub-conscious chords may spring from the text, but go way beyond text, and cannot be put into words.[1]

There are occasions when a new dimension is added to a performance. 'A whole series of perceptions arise. You're consumed with the immediacy, as of a door opening. It is as if one's bones were on fire. Suddenly you're playing something which still has its form, its notes – but it's soaring'.[2] This is the experience as described by an actor but no doubt on such occasions the audience shared in it.

THE ACTOR'S MEANS

Moving and speaking are the means that the actor must learn to use.

Movement

Movement may involve sheer agility, developed so that action is not hampered. It may mean acrobatics, tumbling, fighting, speed, tension, stillness, relaxation and the mobilisation of energy. It means, above all, to express and to respond.

'If you think, you must think with your body'.[3] This involves practice since, for many, thought and action have become separate processes. It also demands the development of what Jane Howell describes as 'a state of hopeful expectancy, without any strain; when everything is together and prepared, and ready to accept something – when it chooses to come'.[4] Her company practised Aikido in order to help them to achieve this condition, which expresses so vividly the state of readiness, brought about by struggles with the medium, which makes it possible for the unpremeditated, illuminating impulse to be manifested and recognised.

[1] Geoffrey Reeves – interview   [2] Neil Johnston – interview
[3] *Towards a Poor Theatre* by Jerzy Grotowski, Methuen
[4] Jane Howell – interview

Similarly, Peter Brook:

> Acting begins with a tiny inner movement so slight that
> it is almost completely invisible. . . . the movement occurs
> in anyone, but in most non-actors the movement is too
> slight to manifest itself in any way. The actor is a more
> sensitive instrument, and in him the tremor is detected.[1]

Peter Brook continues to describe how, in early rehearsals 'the
impulse may get no further than a flicker. . . . For this flicker to
pass into the whole organism, a total relaxation must be there,
either God-given or brought about by work'. This is similar to
Jane Howell's 'state of hopeful expectancy, without any strain'.

The movement of actors is an outcome of the impulse, not
divorced from it, not a mere propulsion of the body from place
to place. Every gesture, every stance, every stillness serves to
illuminate, and is in turn illuminated by, the inner impulse of
feeling.

Geoffrey Reeves in an interview looked forward to a time when:

> We get a performance of Shakespeare which is non-stop
> movement, in which the physical thing is as strong as the
> text and reinforces the text, so that the play is communicable
> to an audience which doesn't understand the text. You get
> near it, of course, in Brook's *Dream*. It was structured in
> that way, it was built on that kind of work.

There are some groups of actors which seem to use movement
as a means of mobilising violent energy; others, often influenced
by Eastern modes such as Aikido and Tai Chi, also build up the
energy which every actor, 'and anybody who is creative', must
develop, but less boisterous, more contained, and more aware –
'trying to come to a more intuitive or empathetic understanding
of the nature of actions, and what can happen, and in what way
people are changed by them'.[2]

Speech

> It is of the utmost importance – and I shall go on repeating
> this – that we learn to speak with the body first and then with
> the voice.[3]

[1] *The Empty Space*, MacGibbon & Kee   [2] Peter Hulton – interview
[3] *Towards a Poor Theatre* by Jerzy Grotowski, Methuen

This statement emphasises the close connection between movement and speech. Speech might be described as breath made into sound; the actor must reach down into his centre for that breath, which supports both action and sound. The quality of the sound which emerges lends both emphasis and meaning to the words spoken and has an impact on the quality of communication.

> How often does one hear voices that do *not* start from deep inside one, which just start from the neck. One can have no commitment to that person because there is so little of him actually working, therefore there is so little of me actually working.[1]

The deep-seated source of speaking is described by Peter Brook:

> A word does not start as a word – it is an end product which begins as an impulse, stimulated by attitude and behaviour which dictate the need for expression.[2]

Of course an actor must practise in order to develop his command of breathing, relaxation and diction but, fundamentally, if the voice is to be expressive it must emerge from depth, and with focus. 'A survivor only needs to sigh and it hits you like a hammer. A commentator could chatter on for a month and you'd get nothing'.[3]

In the act of speaking, the manifestation and reinforcing of the inner impulse is complex involving, as it does, not only what we refer to as the meaning of words, but also the nature of the feeling quality which the voice conveys.

Brook felt a need to revitalise the spoken word. He asked the question:

> Is there another language, just as exacting for the author as a language of words? Is there a language of actions, a language of sounds – a language of word-as-part-of-movement, of word-as-lie, word-as-parody, of word-as-rubbish, of word-as-contradiction, of word-shock or word-cry?[4]

Later, in his International Centre for Theatre Research in Paris, Brook was able to pursue his investigations, and to continue the

---

[1] Keith Yon – interview [2] Brook: op cit
[3] Ted Hughes in an interview quoted in *Orghast at Persepolis* by A. C. H. Smith, Eyre Methuen [4] Brook: op cit

process in the evolution of *Orghast at Persepolis*. The poet, Ted Hughes, had invented, at Brook's request, a language with which to investigate the Prometheus myth 'purged of the haphazard associations of English, which continually tries to supplant experience with the mechanisms of its own autonomous life'.[1]

Orghast was finally evolved in four different languages which were spoken nowhere. A main purpose was to develop relationships between sound and feeling 'in order to do things we could not do in French, English, Parsi. In them we are bound by literal meanings'.[2]

This may sound like an inexcusable attack on language, but it must be remembered that this same director, Brook, was responsible for the superb and illuminating productions of *A Midsummer Night's Dream* and of *King Lear*. Brook writes of the reception of *Lear* in Europe, where:

> the quality of the attention that this audience brought expressed itself in silence and concentration; a feeling in the house that affected the actors as though a brilliant light were turned on their work. As a result the most obscure passages were illuminated; they were played with a complexity of meaning and a fine use of the English language that few of the audience could literally follow, but all could *sense*.[3]

In contrast, in Philadelphia, before an English-speaking audience with different attitudes, the actors 'whipped past those intricate passages that the non-English audience had so enjoyed – which, ironically, only an English-speaking audience could have enjoyed to the full.'[4]

A response to language which will sound surprising to many is described by Leslie Read (a university lecturer). Referring to a passage in *The Winter's Tale*, he says: 'The image is, I suppose, dominated as all images are dominated for me, by my leading sense, which is touch, and the whole thing is physical, and it has all the other qualities that come through that – the kind of squashy, slimy and, at the same time, the warmth of it. There is

[1] Ted Hughes in an interview quoted in *Orghast at Persepolis* by A. C. H. Smith, Eyre Methuen
[2] Peter Brook quoted in *Orghast at Persepolis* by A. C. H. Smith, Eyre Methuen
[3] *The Empty Space* by Peter Brook, MacGibbon & Kee   [4] ibid

humanity there; it's a physical trick thing, so that the image brings to me, three-dimensionally, touch experience. It's there in the rhythms of it'.[1]

> And many a man there is (even at this present,
> Now, while I speake this) holds his Wife by th'Arme
> That little thinkes she ha's been sluyc'd in's absence,
> And his Pond fish'd by his next Neighbor (by
> Sir Smile, his Neighbor:)
>
> *The Winter's Tale*, Act 1, Scene 2

This is very near to Ted Hughes – 'The deeper into language one goes, the less visual/conceptual is its imagery, and the more audial/visceral/muscular its system of tensions'.[2]

All spoken interchanges involve both giving and receiving. It is much easier to give than to receive, easier to speak than to really listen, not only to the words and their feeling quality, but to what is happening between the words and even between syllables.

Even a chairman who sums up 'the sense of the meeting' refers not only to what has been said, but to the overtones of feeling which have accompanied the statements made and which have been expressed in voices, gestures, attitudes and silences.

THE TEXT

> The medium of poetry is WORDS, the medium of drama is people moving about on a stage and using words. That is, the words are only a part of the medium and the gaps between them, or deficiencies in their meaning, can be made up by 'action'.[3]

From words on a printed page actors have to evolve a texture of moving and speaking which illuminate the play, and the pattern of words may, for example, range from *Hamlet* to *The Way of the World*, to Edward Bond's *Saved*, to Beckett's *Endgame*.

[1] Leslie Read – interview
[2] Ted Hughes in notes written for the author and quoted in *Orghast at Persepolis* by A. C. H. Smith, Eyre Methuen
[3] *ABC of Reading* by Ezra Pound, Faber

Clearly, in the professional theatre, many actors are dependent on the director and on his 'reading' of the play. But William Gaskill said:

> The more that I work in theatre the more I think an actor who is working in written drama, with a known play, has to have the ability to *read* a play, has to have the ability to get on the wavelength of the writer, not only to understand what the emotional life of his character is, but to be able to *listen* to the play, so that he knows what is specific about that writer rather than another. I do think that actors are not taught to *read* very well.
>
> To be able to *absorb* the play, to understand the wavelength of it – I find that often terribly inadequate in actors.
>
> Q   Do some actors need to go into action very early, and then go back to the text?
> *WG*   Yes, I think some actors do. But I think we waste a lot of time in rehearsal because the play has not been searched. I find it quite difficult myself because I'd rather get into something than sit around.[1]

He further commented on the importance of the director as 'an intermediary between the actor and the writer' to help the actors to become aware of 'that which is *heard*, the *colour* of the writer's mind, the kind of images he uses, the way he shapes his sentences'.

When he himself reads a text he does not see it visually but feels the emotional flow and the shape of the scenes very strongly. 'When the actors are there, physically there, then the pictures start to exist – in a way you are working with pictures all the time.'

Jane Howell has always found that 'the images derived from words are tactile and visual rather than auditory; the visual and physical sensations of words are very strong'.[2] She found, while at school, indeed from the age of eleven, that she could be instrumental in helping others to understand what was written and explain it, and this capacity led her to become a director in the theatre.

[1] William Gaskill   [2] Jane Howell – interview

Unlike William Gaskill, she finds the visual images that arise from reading a play are of first importance, indeed if the image doesn't come she gets lost and, if possible, doesn't do the play.

> If the image doesn't come the first time it won't come with me. I can't talk myself into it. There is a difference between the image that happens, and the image you calculate on known intellectual facts.

She gives as an example the choice of a circus style for a particular play which, though intellectually justified, didn't work – it was not truly experienced or felt.

The other kind of image that she gets is of rhythms:

> There is a sort of rhythmic drive in some texts and you know that people have to be in certain relationships to reach that moment. It's not a visual thing, but a sort of beat, like a drumbeat. You know once you've heard that, that there's no other way of saying those lines. Pitch I'm not good at; once I've heard the rhythm, that's it.

And she added:

> That's why I loathe working on translated texts; you get meat, but not passion. You don't catch the breath of the man. I prefer adaptations.

Something of the complexities which face the actor in coming to grips with a text of great stature are described by Peter Brook:

> If the actor approaches a speech looking for its form, he must beware not to decide too easily what is musical, what is rhythmic. It is not enough for an actor playing Lear in the storm, to take a running jump at the speeches, thinking of them as splendid slabs of storm music. Nor is it any use speaking them quietly for their meaning on the grounds that they are actually taking place inside his head. A passage of verse can be understood more like a formula carrying many characteristics – in which each letter has a different function. In the storm speeches, the explosive consonants are there to suggest, by imitation, the explosive pattern of thunder, wind and rain. But the consonants are not everything: within these

crackling letters writhes a meaning, a meaning that's ever on the change, a meaning that's carried by meaning's bearer-images. Thus, 'you cataracts and hurricanes spout' is one thing. 'All germens spill at once That make Ingrateful man' is quite another. With writing as compact as this, the last degree of skill is needed: any loud actor can roar both lines with the same noise, but the artist must not only present us with clarity the Hieronymous Bosch-Max Ernst-like image in the second line of the heavens spilling their spermatozoa, he must present this within the context of Lear's own rage. He will observe again that the verse gives great weight to 'That make Ingrateful man', this will reach him as a very precise stage direction from Shakespeare himself, and he will sense and grope for a rhythmic structure that enables him to give to these four words the strength and weight of a longer line and in so doing hurl on the longshot of man in storm a tremendous close-up of his absolute belief in human ingratitude.[1]

In this one passage Brook sets out the elements which the actor has to explore in this brief extract from one speech in the play – the 'crackling consonants', the 'writhing meaning', the 'images', the 'rhythmic structure', the 'weight' of a phrase, the 'longshot', the 'close-up' of belief in human ingratitude, all within the context of Lear's rage and that within the whole tremendous play.

Brook describes this aspect of the process of rehearsal as 'a waltz between director, player and text'. The director is there to 'help the actor to see and overcome his own obstacles. . . . He will know that thought, emotion and body can't be separated, but he will see that a pretended separation must often take place'.[2]

Actors themselves set to work on a text in many different ways. Some, very quickly, get a visual impression and may find this a handicap. Some study the text very closely, and some rely on an instinctive, emotional approach. One actor described how he considered 'crucial points in relation to the character I'm playing. Then, maybe alone, I'll take the seeds of the character into my life, so that in social situations part of me is that character which, at this point, is unformed'.[3] He described how he would take this

[1] *The Empty Space* by Peter Brook, MacGibbon & Kee   [2] ibid
[3] Neil Johnston – interview

preliminary exploration to the first rehearsal and bring in, very cautiously, what he had found.

In order to translate a text into action, in order to act, the actor must get 'turned on' as Geoffrey Reeves expressed it, in order to find the vital energy. With some this results from a very hard, laborious mental process of complete understanding, in which everything is spelt out for themselves slowly. Some recall and relive a personal experience that has moved them, and find their energy from that; and some find a source in fantasy or in imagination.

> You're dealing with the instinctive, the emotional, the unspoken. The great actors have at their command enormous technique, self-control, and the ability to rationalise so that when they have found something they know what processes they have been through and know how to arrive at that point again. It's not all inspiration, but there *is* that jump, and there is no amount of logical hard work and technique which will actually strike the spark – make the lightning jump.[1]

This is, in other words, an account of the expressive process as it has been described earlier in this book. There is the impulse of feeling – 'the instinctive, the emotional, the unspoken', and recognition and recall through its expression in the medium.

CHILDREN

Children do not draw hard and fast lines between dance-like, dramatic, or athletic action and, as discussed on pages 51 and 52, they move very readily from one mode to another.

Drama, which has its roots in action, in the thing done, stems from the impulse to impersonate, to become somebody else, and to enter into various situations. To play a part.

A little girl occupying a Wendy House spends a lot of time dressing up, using an assemblage of garments including a long trailing skirt and high heels. She picks up the 'phone: 'Husband,

[1] Geoffrey Reeves – interview

husband, I'm going to marry you.' She then walks out into the hall where other children are playing, catches hold of a small boy: 'I'm going to marry you.' They walk hand in hand round the room, then she leaves him, goes back into the Wendy House and immediately puts the 'baby' to bed in the cradle.

Her sister had been married during the previous week.

Behind a screen two little girls with two 'victims' (unprotesting), using odds and ends of tin, perform as hairdressers, not only purporting to shampoo, set and comb out the hair, which was in an awful tangle, but also carrying on a conversation with their clients – 'Have you seen Mrs So-and-So?' etc.

Their mothers were hairdressers and, like the 'bride' (who telescoped events with such assurance), these children were assimilating by re-enactment elements in the world about them.

A group of boys make a ring of small bricks, and use hoops and stands to serve as a cage for lions in the circus. Then they crawl into the cage and growl like lions. Nothing else; no tricks; just growling.

The circus had been to town, and to make a structure, to crawl in and growl was a sufficient re-enactment.

A small boy sits on the stage in the school hall with a cloak over his head and remains there for a period of thirty minutes or so.

His intention remains a secret.

These examples are not at all unusual. They were observed in an infant school where time was available in which the children could choose what they wanted to do, and where they had space and a variety of materials to play with. It is characteristic that, with many other children all about them involved in a variety of activities, each could become absorbed in playing out his own concerns.

Most families will be familiar with similar instances, as well as with the more momentary and less specific patterns of sounds and actions which might be described as gallivanting, and which often turn into the enactment of some rôle.

Another and more fully developed example was seen in a small primary school in a West Riding mining village where, during dinner hours, a group of ten year old girls evolved a play, independently of any adults, and proudly showed it to their teacher. The chief character was a naughty boy who got into trouble with his mother and with his teacher, and led the other boys into trouble. His teacher caused him to stand in a corner wearing a dunce's cap.

It seems likely that these girls had envied the adults' acceptance that 'boys will be boys' while the rôle laid down for girls is, usually, a more restricted one. The opportunity to enter into a somewhat storybook version of boys' naughty behaviour was deeply satisfying.

The primary stage

While in infant classes it is quite common to find at least a part of the day set aside for the children's own choice of activity – whether painting, building, reading, writing, dressing-up, acting or what have you, it is unusual to find this practice at the junior stage and yet, where it does happen, it appears to fertilise those activities in which the teacher has a direct hand. Whatever of drama emerges during the period of free choice ('That's when we work,' as one child said) it is something that should be left free to emerge and not guided by the teacher (unless safety is in question), but it is, of course, something to be observed unobtrusively as a valuable indication of the children's concern to identify themselves with the world around them, or with characters in stories or on television.

Children working with a class teacher are less likely to think in terms of subjects than those where, as in secondary schools, every period carries a label. Children do not think in terms of subjects unless they are made to; they use various media – words (spoken, written, sung, shouted), mathematical symbols, paint and clay, movement – and any or all of these are used to explore and extend experience.

Clearly, action is the stuff of drama (a thing done), and it is out of action that, at the primary stage, drama may emerge or, equally, dance may spring, or activity that we know as athletic. Teachers often feel more comfortable if they can label a session as P.E. or Dance or Drama and then activity will have the emphasis the teacher gives it; but children themselves can change readily from one mode to another to suit their purpose. It is important for adults to recognise such changes which are likely, with the youngest children, to be very brief, while with the older ones they will, perhaps, be sustained into episodes.

INTERPLAY

Drama involves, essentially, give and take, action and reaction, inter*play* with others, or with an imagined object. Thus a child needs to have sufficient expressive experience himself (able to inter-relate impulse and medium) if he is to engage in exchanges with another so that both are able to modify each other's attitudes and actions. Where expressive resources are meagre and unstable there can be no real interplay, only a perfunctory going through the motions of an exchange, often accompanied by mere chatter and giggles of embarrassment. Indeed embarrassment is a sure sign that a situation is too much at that moment for a child (or for that matter an adult) to manage, and there may well be a need to strengthen individual resources, or to engage in encounters of a simpler, and perhaps more momentary, kind.

Left to themselves, children usually evolve patterns (that may be called dramatic) in very small groups, twos, threes or fours. This is how, also, they play with a football or at cricket, because they can manage the give and take that the situation demands. If the group is too large the situation becomes confused and even chaotic. For example, in a school hall a number of groups were working on stories of their choice. It happened that side by side with a group of five 9–10 year olds (two boys, three girls) who had just evolved a magical Death of Arthur, was a group of about ten trying to work out the episode of the Sword in the Stone but unable to resolve it. 'Too many came,' they said; and they were right. The group was too large, and the individual expressive resources insufficient, for the children to be able to respond to each other. They could give, but not receive, and so there was no true interplay.

The Death of Arthur, in which the five children used almost a quarter of the large space, was very remarkable. They had decided who should be Arthur, and who Sir Bedivere, and their choice seemed perfect; they appeared to know who could most readily embody their feeling for these two characters. The three girls who, it emerged, were to be the three queens, and more besides, knelt close together with heads bowed, in a triangular shape with one of its 'sides' opening towards what was presently to be established as the shore, some distance away. Sir Bedivere helped the failing Arthur to the edge of the mere (at once established quite clearly for the children themselves and for the onlookers) and was ordered to bear the sword, Excalibur, and hurl it into the mere. He carried the sword away (again this was perfectly clear), but handling it and admiring it he became reluctant, and finally hid it. He returned to the king, who perceived the lie, and ordered him again to throw the sword into the mere. Again Sir Bedivere, torn between the beauty of the sword, the lake and the king's command, could not obey, and again he hid the sword. Once more he returned to the king and lied, and the king, summoning up his remaining energy, with great urgency ordered him to obey. This time Bedivere uncovered the sword, took it, whirled it round his head and flung it far into the lake. And a hand reached up and drew it down. (At that breathingtaking moment three separate observers each saw the surface and colour of the lake, though they did not discover their mutual experience until much later that day.) Bedivere returned to Arthur, and helped him to stand erect. Slowly, upright, the king walked towards the three kneeling figures, who rose; he entered among them and together, slowly, they all sank.

All this was done with exquisite clarity and assurance. Once the group had formed and decided on their story there was no discussion; the whole was evolved in action. Each child was able both to express his own feeling for the story and also to deepen his recognition of that feeling in response to what was manifested by others.

These children carried out the action between King Arthur and Sir Bedivere literally, but in the second part of the episode they used symbolic form of a high order. The three girls embodied the three queens, the barge and the departure to Avalon, and from their group the arm emerged to draw Excalibur down into the lake. One can imagine how fussy this might have been, with a barge coming alongside, and so on. Moreover the children knew, not analytically, but in their bones, how to evolve dramatic form from a literary story.

This achievement was the more impressive because of the failure alongside them of the group trying to evolve the Sword in the Stone – 'Too many came.' Yet how many children would know, as they did, why it went wrong and would, consequently, learn how to manage themselves.

Another, and much less developed, example of readiness to respond to each other occurred when suddenly, while the whole class was working individually, a boy began to struggle desperately with a wild horse. It reared and he was lifted off the ground; it tore down the room and the boy with it; it charged all over the place and, mostly, the boy, trying vainly to throw his weight against the halter, had to follow – often losing his balance and almost falling. At first the other members of the class merely got out of the way, then they joined in and became involved in the violent to and fro. The incident happened 'out of the blue', and the extraordinary agility of the boy made it possible for him to create the horse not only for himself, but for everybody in the room, and the children were able, spontaneously, to give and take in the game.

Another vivid example of understanding one's own impulse in the light of the expressive actions of others is given on page 19, where a nine year old found it impossible to face the townspeople in *The Pied Piper*. This same boy, as he left the street, ran his hand along the low balustrade of a bridge, creating it quite clearly both for himself and all those present.

The cheapjack trying to sell vases to a critical (in the vernacular) crowd, the witty version of a cricket match, Perseus taking to the air and destroying the Gorgon reflected in his shield, all showed children able to be lit up by an inner impulse, to respond in action that was clear and which in turn reinforced and developed the impulse so that new characters and situations were explored. Moreover, they were able to recognise and share in an interplay between their own and others' impulses and actions, often with actual persons, but also creating and responding to an imagined person or object.

Interplay in twos is as much as some can manage; to work in

threes is not only more complex but, of course, quite different –
two *against* one, one *between* two, one *leading* two, and so on. It
takes a lot of experience before, in a threesome, the initiative can
be passed from one to another.

And four is different again – apt to become two couples, or
just four individuals in a huddle, like four small boys with a
football – each gets the ball if he can. The children discover
themselves in action, seize upon and develop an idea in action –
maybe it lasts two minutes, maybe much longer. If they need
preliminary discussion, or action degenerates into discussion, the
likelihood is that something is awry. 'Too many came.'

When the time seems ripe for the whole class to be involved
in some sort of composition, it is first of all very important for
the teacher to help the children to conceive of the story or theme
in terms of space and action, that is, in a dramatic and not
literary form. Many children have been handicapped by their
teacher's and their own failure to grasp this. Then, if the teacher
is not to manipulate the whole thing, the children need to build
it up very gradually. So, for example, in *The Pied Piper* they all
work hard to become rats (and some superb ones are likely to
emerge), they all become Pied Pipers, and some compelling ones
discover themselves where, too often, there are only pretty
clichés. Then a Pied Piper and a small group of rats work
together; and so on. On the way to building up a Jabberwock
many Jabberwocks are invented, and everybody experiments
with becoming mimsy borogroves and mome raths. At first
every child is a Perseus killing the Gorgon. Small groups become
the three queer sisters with the single eye, or the three gods
investing Perseus with the magic sandals, sword and shield.
Everybody is Beowolf fighting Grendel; everybody is one of a
pile of dry bones coming gradually to life, everybody becomes the
Four Winds in turn; much much later an Ezekiel emerges and the
whole pattern is worked out, each individual and each group
playing their part. It may be a whole term or a whole year before
the various elements are ready to come together. Generally the
smaller incidents are greater than the whole, but there come times
when the class has a need to build something together. If there
are onlookers, they are best disposed of as unobtrusively as

84

possible at the edges and corners of the working space, so that the presence of outsiders does not tempt any child to 'put on an act' and so that the essential expressive experience is continued.

SOUNDS AND WORDS

The vocal sound that bursts out of a leap is quite different from that which explodes from the stamp of a foot, different again from that which is forced out of a squeeze, or from the gentler sounds that emerge from tapping, or stroking or swaying. With children the association of action and sound is unmistakable, and they are very ready to be helped to explore further; in adults it is usually, at least in England, damped down, but nevertheless present. The term 'gesture' is used not only in connection with ostensible action but also with the inflexions of speech, which are dependent upon the breath vibrating through the vocal cords, pharynx and mouth, and the actions of tongue, lips and palates.

Children explore language in terms of chatter and conversation (as well, of course, as in reading and writing), but they also need to deepen the natural association between action and sound and to discover how the same word can have different meanings. This may well have a beginning in nonsense sounds. For example, Jubjub Birds, in the Jabberwocky, have conversations in pairs and the use of nonsense sounds conveys, very clearly, the kind of creature they have each become – petulant, greedy, wary, aggressive – and as they encounter another strange creature, and another, their own 'speech' changes as they recognise and respond to the characteristics of the other birds. Many vivid exchanges are carried out through the medium of nonsense sounds. A group of boys became monkeys who found a drum in the jungle and did not know what to make of it until, accidentally, they made a sound with it, and soon a young and particularly impudent monkey connected a stick with the drum and began to 'play' it. This whole incident was uproariously funny; it changed every time the boys played it and they played it many times until it ceased to change, went dead and was dropped.

Words may, of course, be used experimentally and expressively in the same way, and as the quality, and so the meaning of, for example, 'Come!' changes, different situations arise.

A group of children used the word 'Rain', which emerged in the first place from their actions and attitudes of waiting, then of anxious searching, followed by a climax and chorus of urgent appeal, which turned to silence with the realisation of the first half-felt drops, then a second climax of exultation: 'It's raining!' So was created, through sound and action, a complete, if brief, dramatic sequence with a 'text' of great economy and full of meaning.

Play with sounds, and with the varying sounds of words and the imitation of accents, led to an extraordinary number of versions of, for example, *Three Blind Mice*, in which the rhythm of the lines was kept, but the sounds changed with amazing and amusing results. When Russia put the first man into space his welcome by Kruschev and the crowd, and his own description of space, were done with immense verve in 'Russian'. The changing emotional content of the speeches (Kruschev's, the mother's, Gagarin's description of space) was perfectly clear.

In connection with his invented language 'Orghast', Ted Hughes wrote:

The deeper into language one goes, the more dominated it becomes by purely musical modes, and the more dramatic it becomes – the more unified with total states of being and with the expressiveness of physical action.[1]

He describes the impact of his invented language on the actors:

It released the actors in some interesting ways. When they have a new sound which has no precise intellectual content, they have to search their resources for an actuality which will give it content – unless they are just going to make an empty noise. They search for the most living feeling in them at that moment – a feeling that might have been evoked by imagination, by their precise situation in dramatic action, or just by their life. They can't short-circuit into the given meaning of words and evade the real issue. The real issue is to confront their whole response to that moment.[2]

[1] *Orghast at Persepolis* by A. C. H. Smith, Eyre Methuen   [2] ibid

These statements would appear to illuminate the process by which the children described above, through their rich play with sounds and words, relate sound and feeling, discover new meanings for words, and also develop their capacity to respond to words. The process is also related to experiences of touching, tasting and seeing.

> You become more and more conscious about the colour of
> words, the taste of words, the shape of words. You acquire
> a sense of discrimination and for me this discrimination
> starts with movement, and it comes into writing, speaking,
> painting.[1]

Alongside these experiences there may well be encounters between characters from the children's own surroundings with conversations in the vernacular. These may be brief (less than sixty seconds) when only two characters are concerned, but nevertheless showing a sense of development from the opening gambit relating to the weather to the culmination: 'Well, ah'd better be goin', Ah've got ter get our Freddy's dinner in't oven. Ta-ta luv. See you aafter.'

The frustrations of a visit to the seaside are recalled in a group dialogue lasting just under two minutes:

Mother: Ow my poor feet; they're crippling me.
Father: Well Ah told yer not to put them shoes on.
Son: Nobody cares about me, and it's lookin' a bit dull at that.
Mother: Ah wish you'd shoot oop.
Father: It's a wunder our Sheila didn't want to go on't donkeys.
Mother: Ah doan't care whether she wants to go on't donkeys or not; she's not goin' on.
Son: When can Ah go ter Bingo?
Mother: Bingo! Is that all you think about? We've only joost coom.
Aunt: It were a luvely camera ee wun laast year Minnie, and ee took a luvley picture of me an all.

[1] Bessie Bullough – interview

Mother: Ah doan't care wot e wun, ee's not goin' now.
           Where's my spectacles?
Aunt: They were in't baasket before we coom.
Mother: Well they're not there now.
Father: Our Mary had 'em laast.
Daughter: Ah haven't doon it.
Mother: Ah haven't got them in me pocket.
Son: Is this what you're lookin' for?
Mother: Well, what do you think it is, yer silly fool!
Son: Ah wish we'd never coom.
Father: Shoot oop will yer.
Aunt: It's goin' to raain.
Son: Ah told yer. Where's t' shelter?
Mother: Nobody's comin' under *my* umbrella.
Several voices: Nobody wants ter.[1]

One group of children included the play of Pyramus and Thisbe
from *A Midsummer Night's Dream* in their own version of a May
festival, which began with the carrying in and erection of the
maypole to the critical comments of those assembled: 'It's nowt
so good as laast year.' 'It's not straaight.' After the acrobats,
whose antics also evoked comments, came the players, some of
whom became involved with the crowd:

Moonshine: This lanthorn doth the hornéd moon present.
Onlooker: Ah doan't think it looks a bit laake moon.
Moonshine: (put out) This lanthorn doth the hornéd moon
            present.
Onlooker: Ah still doan't think it looks a bit laake moon.
Moonshine: (with almost threatening emphasis) This
            lanthorn *doth the hornéd moon present.*
Onlooker: (not really acquiescing, but tolerant) Arl raight
            then.

But while children enjoy their own vernacular, as well as picking
up the accents of others, they can always 'suit the word to the
action'; thus, when they become gods their speech becomes
godlike (also apt to become a little stilted).

In one school a whole class of boys who were lit up in the

[1] Tape recording made in course of action

first place by the disc 'Dem Bones, Dem Dry Bones', went on to develop the story of Ezekiel. 'There is no life in these bones, O Lord,' and the Lord, making a funnel of his hands, and invisible to the group: 'There shall be life,' with almost matter of fact assurance. But not less than the words spoken clearly and movingly, the boys took enormous pleasure in making the extraordinary sounds of the bones coming together, and the groups who evolved the Four Winds in movement and sound evoked the howling north, the bitter edge of the east, the gentler west, and for the south the sounds of summer, full of bees humming. Finally Ezekiel passed through the living multitude and led them forth – an exceeding great army – to an act of prayer and worship.

These boys were members of a mining community. Their resources in movement were remarkable and often more dance-like than dramatic. Many of the boys were wonderfully agile, but a spastic, from crouching in a corner, was able, gradually, to emerge and share with the rest and, finally, to enjoy the centre of a very crowded space. Mostly these boys were skinny, but at one stage four very fat boys were members of the class; they learnt to manage and to exploit their roundness, and incidents were evolved (for example, they formed the four wheels of a racing car and each in turn rolled away, leaving the driver stranded) in which the rest of the class had great pride and pleasure.

The children referred to in this chapter were able to express and recognise in themselves many different feelings – vigorous, violent, lusty, gentle, comical; and to relate to and understand such feelings in others in the interplay which is characteristic of drama. They were able to bring to vivid life the people among whom they lived, and whom they observed, as well as to enter into many characters and events drawn from the stories and poems they had read. In doing so they extended their experience. Quite often extraordinary moments of penetration seemed to happen 'out of the blue'. Such moments cannot be predicted or planned, they can only be made possible by a variety of means – through warm and confident relationships with each other and with their teacher, through a gradual and subtle development of resources, through a rich texture of experience through the senses, and by means of a constant response to and understanding of the inner impulse manifested, reinforced and remembered through use of the expressive medium.

The secondary stage

THE NEEDS OF ADOLESCENTS

The actor has himself as his field of work. This field is richer than that of the painter, richer than that of the musician, because to explore he needs to call on every aspect of himself. His hand, his eye, his ear, and his heart are what he is studying and what he is studying with.[1]

One might, equally, state that the *adolescent* has himself as his field of work, and that the arts of dance and of drama have considerable potential for exploration, and for achieving integration during a phase of development when his sense of identity is threatened. The references made earlier in this chapter to the development of actors are highly relevant to the development of adolescents, who find themselves in a world where objective aims and values pre-dominate, but where the experience of the inner self, of sensate experience, is ignored or feared. 'Who am I? Where am I going? These questions are asked and adults often do too little to help them find the answers'.[2]

'The dominant fear in my childhood was the fear of not getting a job. The dominant fear of youngsters now is the fear of anonymity'.[3]

In England, boys and girls enter the secondary stage of education at eleven or at thirteen; this follows a phase of comparative certainty and self-assurance. They then enter into a stage of development when they become increasingly aware of objectives that the world seems to find acceptable and desirable, but which seem to be beyond their reach. Their former, secure sense of identity, of knowing who they are and where they stand, is shaken, even shattered. A few can rate themselves as successful in academic terms (they do well in examinations), and all, whether they fail or succeed, are geared to the kind of objective assessment

[1] *The Empty Space* by Peter Brook, MacGibbon & Kee
[2] C. J. Gill – interview   [3] Barry Willcock, headmaster – interview

which the modern world demands, and so to a curriculum which places little emphasis on the understanding and management of those sensations and feelings by which the individual is stirred and energised.

The situation is not made any easier by the current use of the blanket term 'teenager' – almost as if this were synonymous with 'adolescent'. Its use lumps together a number of age groups and may well prevent recognition of the stage of growth and development known as adolescence so that neither the early, or late, maturity of individuals is discerned.

The very term 'drama' has, for many teachers, a connotation of crisis, not necessarily related to timetabled drama periods, but to events in school where encounters between pupil and pupil, or between themselves and their pupils, have become explosive, and savour, strongly, of the dramatic. When, on top of this, periods given to drama are regarded, not always without reason, as episodes of noisy release, it is not surprising that the potentialities of this art for 'people behaving as a whole', 'the sensitive inter-relation between people working confidently together', and the time taken to 'create awareness of other people without competitiveness' are not realised. These phrases are extracted from the statements included earlier in the section on the training of actors, and seem highly relevant to the personal development of young people, to which drama in schools could contribute so much.

ARRANGEMENTS IN SCHOOL

Circumstances usually make such development almost impossible to achieve.

> In my first teaching job, English and drama in a boys'
> school, and in the first term – it always happens, of course –
> I was given the fourth year leavers, thugs, thirty of them,
> on a Friday afternoon, all the afternoon. I was told: 'You
> can do drama with them.' 'Fine. Where?' 'In the classroom;
> and you might like to use these – *Six Plays for Boys*'.[1]

This teacher continued to discuss:

> The limitations of the lesson for forty minutes: kids coming
> in (often from different classes and different parts of the

[1] Roger Sell – interview

school) and after ten minutes gradually getting down to some work, building up something, having to stop early, and then not seeing the group for another week. It happens all the time. It takes an incredibly good and sensitive teacher to be able, under the usual circumstances, to be able, even a little bit, to open up children in a way that means something later on.

This kind of pattern (although some different ones are beginning to emerge) is a common one; not only is it almost impossible to establish work in any depth in the time available (a net thirty minutes is the most that can be expected), but, even more important, this may be the sole encounter in the week between the teacher and a particular class. Under these circumstances it is only after a period of time, perhaps two years, that the kind of relationship can be established in which the children feel free to work with sensitivity. It is perhaps necessary to repeat that in drama, the thing done, where the person is both instrument and medium, 'it's the behaviour that makes conscious what they are doing'.[1] Perhaps, above all, adolescents need to know that they are known, but too often the pattern of the school week, and the many staff changes, mean that they know, only too well, that they are not.

Not only may the drama lesson be the single encounter between the teacher and a particular class, but the teacher may be expected to work with a different group for every period of his working week – maybe thirty periods, maybe more. The strain must be tremendous.

DIRECTOR/TEACHER

In *The Empty Space*, Peter Brook writes of some of the ways in which a director must work, and although the reference is to the realisation of a play in the theatre, it also illuminates teaching – which, indeed, directing is.

> The director must look for where the actor is messing up his own right urges – and here he must help the actor to see and overcome his own obstacles. All this is a dialogue and a dance between director and player. A dance is an accurate

[1] Barry Willcock – interview

metaphor, a waltz between director, player and text. Progression is circular, and deciding who's the leader depends on where you stand.

There is a place for discussion, for research, for the study of history and documents as there is a place for roaring and howling and rolling on the floor. Also there is a place for relaxation, informality, chumminess, but also there is a time for silence and discipline and intense concentration. Before his first rehearsal with our actors Grotowski asked for the floor to be swept and for all clothes and personal belongings to be taken out of the room. Then he sat behind a desk, speaking to the actors from a distance, allowing neither smoking nor conversation. This tense climate made certain experiences possible.[1]

There is much more of value to any teacher, but especially (in a final quotation from the same chapter), the statement that the help given to the actor is to try to ensure that he will:

. . . bring into being an unconscious state of which he is completely in charge. The result is whole, indivisible – but emotion is continually illuminated by intuitive intelligence so that the spectator, though wooed, assaulted, alienated and forced to re-assess, ends by experiencing something equally indivisible. *Catharsis can never have been simply an emotional purge: it must have been an appeal to the whole man.* (my italics)

NEED TO DEVELOP INDIVIDUAL RESOURCES
It is only natural that children should see in their drama period an opportunity for release. They spend much of the day sitting behind desks, reading, writing, speaking (but not much), and it is only in the gymnasium, on the playing field, or in the room given to drama, that they are released into space. The ways in which the gymnasium and the playing field are used are more or less defined and the parts to be played (as it were) are more or less accepted. In both gymnastics and games, skill is a quality to be aimed at, very often of a specific kind, and in the course of a week more time is usually made available for these activities than for drama.

[1] *The Empty Space* by Peter Brook, MacGibbon & Kee

So, very easily, drama can be regarded as a bit of a lark ('A fun thing which the teacher is always trying to make too serious'[1]) and if the attitude of the drama teacher is very different from that of most of the rest of the staff (as is quite likely), the younger children, especially, are apt to arrive in a carefree way, buzzing like bees and, like bees, swarming over the space.

While such exuberance may well be exploited in activities of an acrobatic nature which demand the skilful management of weight, it is essential for each one to learn to be able to work individually, with concentration, on himself, so that he begins, if only for short spans, to experience the oscillation between the inner, feeling impulse, and the action into which it emerges and which, in turn, reinforces the impulse. In this way each one begins to strike roots from which further growth is possible. This, also, is release, but highly individual, and not merely as a member of an exuberant mob. The need to establish individual resources before a group, or even a pair, can manage the give and take which interplay demands, has been referred to on pages 80 and 82. It is easier to develop in a class where, as in a primary school, the children know each other and their teacher well, and where drama may grow naturally out of other concerns instead of being a single 'outing' unconnected with the rest of the week. Nevertheless, unless individual resources are established in some depth, drama will make only a superficial contribution to the children's ability to manage, and to extend in range and subtlety, their life of feeling.

This individual exploration may take place in terms of movement. For example, the experience of feeling oneself firm and resistant to pressure can be achieved by the pressing of feet, hands and other parts of the body against the floor or some other surface, or even by pressing the feet, hands and other parts of the body against each other. Alternatively, a feeling of the lightest possible touch can be similarly achieved, especially if the eyes are closed. It is easier to achieve close concentration with movements that are slow rather than quick and with actions that are directed inwards towards the body rather than those which are directed outwards. This does not mean, of course, that the experience of movement should be limited, but it is useful to understand not

[1] Liz Mantle – written answer to questionnaire

only how to help children to become absorbed but also how different modes of movement may be used to help, for example, those who find it difficult to be other than slow or heavy or excitable.

The involvement of the self may well be centred on some image; for example, the entry and progress into a deep cave, and the return to light and space; or concentration on a pool, gradually evoking its surface, its size and surroundings, and objects beneath the surface. Departure from the pool may be brought about, perhaps, by an arrival, by the distant striking of a clock or some other sound, or merely by the feeling that 'it was time to go'. On one occasion when two men were able to share the image they presently got up and went to another part of the room; they explained later: 'The water was too muddy; we couldn't make it clear.' Their communication with each other had been wordless.

A group in which the individuals had never learnt to focus began to work within themselves when they each had a chair, and started to examine it through handling it in all sorts of ways, feeling shapes and surfaces, turning it into different objects and becoming thoroughly intimate with it. They moved away trying to keep the image in mind, then they returned to see how closely they had managed this. When, after moving away and trying to retain the image, they relinquished it, they discovered that at that moment they spontaneously started to move faster.

Soon they began to hold conversations with their chair, using nonsense sounds. They were able to sustain these occasions quite easily for twenty minutes or more. They found in this experience relief in a playlike activity, but were also able to build up an inner concentration and confidence and, presently, to explore situations with a partner imaginatively and sensitively.

Naturally, during all these processes, as in others, reinforcement by the teacher is essential.

In his teaching there is a great deal of subtle reinforcement going on the whole time. It often comes from bodily posture, gesture, voice and relationship, even more than in what is said. And this gives you confidence to go on; it makes you more open to the experience which he, as

teacher, has devised. And since you have that confidence
that you're not going to be snubbed or discouraged, you
are able to go on and explore. You're exploring yourself in
relation to the medium; then this subtle reinforcement
urges you again even further and to test out your resources
even more deeply. And as you find that you have these
resources, there is this self-revelation, and again you have
confidence.[1]

There could hardly be a clearer description of the purpose of
drama as well as of the teaching process, but it does not fit in at
all readily with the brief weekly period that is customary in many
schools.

The actor's means have been described as moving and speaking,
and these are similarly the means whereby children explore
themselves, make contact with others, and penetrate a written
text.

MOVEMENT

All children have some experience of movement in the field of
physical education and games. Boys who play soccer or basket-
ball have considerable experience of give and take and the use of
space; they also know what it is to move three-dimensionally and
with agility. Their gymnastics, too, have probably encouraged
them to manage their weight in all sorts of acrobatic skills. Some
of the games played by girls, especially netball and lacrosse, have
strong three-dimensional qualities, and again gymnastics will be
concerned with the management of their own weight, with
agility and flexibility.

All such skill, all such activity, and all the interplay that is
characteristic of games, provide a valuable background to drama;
but such movement is, quite properly, objective – the ball is hit,
thrown or kicked with the purpose of scoring a goal, and in
gymnastics the body is an object to be manipulated. In schools
where dance is included (in some, even in some boys' schools, it is
an integral part of the drama lesson) the children bring to drama
experience of movement that is expressive, that is to say, the form
which it takes stems from and in turn reinforces, the inner
impulse of feeling.

[1] C. J. Gill – interview

It follows that while there are strong similarities between the actions experienced in games and gymnastics and the action demanded by drama (for example, accelerating, slowing down, changing direction, awareness of space and the agile management of the weight of the body) the major difference lies, in expressive movement, in the concentration on the stuff of movement itself.

> If you become interested in the quality of *how* you move, then you go inwards, not outwards, and you find yourself in the world of yourself, and the imaginative world and the world of yourself are one. When you come into drama and into dance you are no longer concerned with an outside purpose, you are concerned with the whole of yourself.[1]

For example, travelling across a space (perhaps from diagonally opposite corners of a room) acquires a different emphasis if the whole attention is focused on the space ahead, on *arriving*, rather than on merely travelling. In turn, the experience is quite different if, when traversing the same space, attention is focused on the place left behind, on *leaving*. These two different experiences may serve, when they are fully incorporated, as a foundation for the idea of 'escape' – escaping *from*, and escaping *to*, with the balance of attention shifting from one to the other. Places of hiding and phases of exposure between them may begin to emerge from this fundamental pattern, and these situations may gradually build up to become more detailed; for example, a high, narrow hiding place may become a tree, while crouching low creates a bush or a rock. Listening and looking add further dimensions to the pattern.

This kind of development stemming, as it does, from action elements, is likely to build up a clear, dramatic pattern with a considerable degree of self-involvement, whereas preparation through discussion is apt to emerge as a verbalised 'story', full of detail perhaps, but lacking in dynamic and dramatic quality.

As resources become richer and stronger, and the capacity for self-involvement deepens, such an episode may be shared in pairs, or in small groups, but at first it is best pursued individually.

At a much later stage different circumstances of *leaving* can be built up in twos who discover, through action and attitude,

[1] A. R. Stone – interview

whether the one who is leaving is merely returning to his home across the road, going much further away before returning, or leaving and not expecting to return. Words are not necessary, images of time and distance can be communicated without their use and without any gestures that might be called 'mime'.

In this latter example gesture and stillness are elements which help to build up awareness – awareness both of oneself and of the other person. Communication through gesture is built up, in part, by concentration on different parts of the body. For example, a turn of the head, which is initiated by a movement of the eyes, is a different experience from a movement where the glance follows *after* the head. There is yet another considerably different experience when attention is focused on an ear and in turning the ear seems to lead. Tension and a slight movement of withdrawal in the spine, a hand raised with the palm, or with the back, uppermost, emphasis on the knees or the elbows, bring about different experiences as long as such actions are used to explore deeply, and do not become exercises.

Stillness, too, needs to be experienced, as having many different qualities and not merely as an interruption in action. It is always charged with action, action of which it is the outcome, or action which is to emerge from it.

Jane Howell refers to one very important kind of stillness:

> The time of waiting for the moment of instinct, when there was a state which I described as nothingness, or relaxation which is not collapse, but a state of hopeful expectancy without any strain. When everything is together and prepared and ready to accept something. When it chooses to come.[1]

IN TOUCH

We speak of being 'in touch', or 'out of touch', meaning 'in contact' or 'not in contact', neither expression being taken literally, but signifying a quality of communication. When we say we are 'touched', or that some event was 'very touching', then a dimension of warmth and sympathy is added.

The literal experience of touching may act as an important foundation for the development of that which Grotowski refers

[1] Jane Howell – interview

to as contact which 'changes all relationship, and it is also the secret of harmony between men'.[1]

It may begin with the handling of objects or the touching of surfaces. Sometimes, keeping the eyes closed, the experience may be described verbally to a partner; or gestures alone may be used to convey shape, surface, weight, softness or hardness. To this can be added the practice of just *not* touching a surface with different parts of the body. This develops a very strong quality of attention towards the object.

Work with a partner may start in very practical ways; for example by moving a partner's limbs so that different shapes are made; by following or leading a partner exactly; by so-called trust exercises in which one is responsible for lowering, catching, manipulating the weight of a partner safely. Practice in mirroring a partner's actions, in receiving exactly an imagined object, or the imagined ball, all help to make unselfconscious but close contact, although when an imagined object is used attention to the partner himself is slightly diverted.

Forms of combat without contact demand close attention and considerable agility and skill.

There comes a stage when two move together just not touching each other and this can establish gentle and intimate relationships without embarrassment.

In a more complex situation a partner uses part of the room to create, without words, but by his glance, attitude and few gestures a particular space – its dimensions and its nature. As soon as the space is established for him his partner joins him and shares it. The experience can be surprisingly clear and vivid images are communicated without speech.

When children reach the secondary stage without having any previous experience of drama, it is especially difficult for boys and girls to work together; indeed it is very usual to see boys working at one end of the room and girls at the other, and for each to have a degree of contempt for the others' interests. It might make for more progress if they worked separately, for a year, perhaps for two, until they had sufficiently deep-seated resources and confidence to make working together stimulating rather than embarrassing. There is certainly a period in early

[1] *Towards a Poor Theatre* by Jerzy Grotowski, Methuen

adolescence when boys and girls of the same age show little sympathy towards each other.

As with primary school children, the size of group that can work together can only be increased as individuals develop resources which enable them not only to give, but to receive, the intimations of others.

One large group, at a rather elementary stage of development, was able to work together in a gamelike situation. All members of it, except one, were disposed sitting or lying, individually, scattered over the floor. The one figure sat at a table on a low platform at the end of the room, reading a book. The members of the group began to catch each other's eyes, presently to murmur and to move towards each other. When the 'captain' raised his eyes from the book the rule of the game was that everyone had to freeze. Gradually the smaller groups got bigger, the sounds louder and the glances of the 'captain' began to be directed against them. But the game of freeze and action continued until one large group had been formed when a series of movements and rushes towards the 'captain' began. These developed into a final assault which seemed likely to overwhelm him, but at the last moment he suddenly stood, and with a gesture and a single word – 'Look!' – changed their action and attention to the opposite direction and they began to move away from him and towards this new focus. The whole episode retained its fundamental pattern, but became the rebellion of the crew against Christopher Columbus' intention of continuing his voyage to the west. The word 'Look!' became 'Land'!' and the rebellious crew, having sighted it, knelt and crossed themselves in thanksgiving.

Within this simple, game-like form, they had to learn to work together, to build up tension and action gradually, to give Columbus a chance to function, not to rush him too suddenly, and build up a response between themselves and him.

SPEAKING

A word does not start as a word – it is an end product which begins as an impulse, stimulated by attitude and behaviour which dictate the need for expression.[1]

[1] *The Empty Space* by Peter Brook, MacGibbon & Kee

In most infant classrooms there is usually a lot of talking, not by any means always conversation, though the give and take of real exchanges does happen, arising out of what is going on, or out of some excitement at home. The teacher insinuates herself into this process, and talking with an adult is an important element in the development of language and of sociability.

At the secondary stage the situation is very different. Children usually spend a great deal of time behind desks, and the opportunities for exchanges between a teacher and some thirty pupils are often limited to question and answer, while talking between pupils too often stems from inattention to the matter in hand and so must be suppressed. But times are changing and James Britton writes:

> Perhaps the most important general implication for teaching, however, is to note that anyone who succeeded in outlawing talk in the classroom would have outlawed life for the adolescent.[1]

Drama, although rooted in action, naturally emerges into the spoken word, and develops into an increasing readiness to use and shape language, to find words, and to use them expressively.

The same process is involved, impulse and medium react the one on the other, the medium being not only words but the voice.

> It is a two-way process, and a rather marvellous one, you know what you want to communicate, but in the physical act of making sound, meanings take on a new dimension.[2]

Confidence and expressiveness may be stimulated in the first place by the use of sounds and of invented words to carry a situation – Brook's 'language of actions, a language of sounds'.[3]

Imitation of sounds, for example, of a rainstorm, of the street, of machines, and of other languages and regional accents, all develop flexibility in the use of sound. The process also involves listening with attention, and there may be phases of silence within the room during which the members of the class notice and collect, between them, all outside sounds heard within a period of five minutes.

[1] *Language and Learning* by James Britton, Allen Lane/The Penguin Press   [2] *Voice and the Actor* by Cicely Berry, Harrap
[3] *The Empty Space* by Peter Brook, MacGibbon & Kee

Naturally there must be situations which light up the need to communicate, whether by sounds alone or through words – an argument, the relating of some exciting incident, a description of oneself or one's partner, or of some object within the room without identifying it by name.

> Most people think of speech as something of extremity – just as one would touch with one's finger tips.[1]

As described on page 85, exploration of the changing meanings in a single word, even conversations built up from different intonations of the same word, help to bring about speaking that is rooted in some depth, not 'as something of extremity'. For example, 'No' and 'Where' can carry many shades of meaning, and brief sentences such as 'This is the way' very easily build up into episodes in which sound and action are fused and convey a variety of situations.

That which is heard has an impact on the way in which the voice is used:

> The voice is the most intricate mixture of what you hear, how you hear it, and how you unconsciously choose to use it in the light of your personality and experience.[2]

Teachers know very well that screaming begets screaming, and shouting incites shouting. At the other extreme we all know that we respond to somebody who has lost his voice and whispers, by whispering too. We know, too, that children who move to an area where the general quality of speech is different, for example English children who move to Wales, are very quickly infected by the new 'tune'.

The quality of sound in a school (and the mode of movement about the school) says much about the quality of communication in that school. There are, for example, schools where meals must be eaten in silence, others where noise rises and rises, and the staff battle against it. There are also schools where the level of conversation is civilised. The roots of this condition lie deep in the nature of the relationships between adults and children, and between the children themselves.

[1] Keith Yon – interview   [2] Berry: op cit

In drama, listening is perhaps not sufficiently emphasised, and the impact of voice upon voice not fully realised.

TEXT

A text brings another creative force.[1]

The exploration of a text by a dramatist of quality can be an enlarging and exhilarating experience, especially if it emerges naturally from all that has gone before, so that the children are not flattened by the encounter with the written word, but can get it off the page, mastering its rhythms, responding to its images, and penetrating its meanings. Above all, the readiness to respond to another's text must be such that the inner impulse is not quenched, but emerges as the word in action. This means that the children not only make the dramatist's words their own, but they have to receive and respond to his words spoken by others.

Improvisation will often continue to be a means of coming to grips with situations in a text. For example, the opening exchanges in *Hamlet* may well be based on an improvisation in which soldiers on guard duty in intense darkness, and on edge, challenge mistakenly, reassure each other and change duties.

It may well be that texts of quality seem to be beyond the children's reach; but it is very possible to develop a version using the events of the play, including passages as written, but set in a pattern of action and words that have been improvised.

> I usually have a considerable dialogue with a text when I read it. Sometimes this is so strong that in a number of cases a different thing comes from that dialogue. This occurred with *Antigone* and whatever I had to do with *Beowulf*.[2] There are two different things. One is the response to the text, which emerges in something new; the other is to see the text and allow it to fulfil its implications.[3]

It is also possible to study, within a particular theme, a series of encounters in a number of plays. For example, 'Encounters with Death' from *Everyman* through Shakespeare and Ibsen to the present day. Similarly, perhaps, 'The Brothers', from Cain and Abel onwards.[4]

[1] Roger Seil – interview
[3] Peter Hulton – interview
[2] A performance evolved round the Old English heroic poem
[4] See *The Primal Curse* by Honor Matthews, Chatto & Windus

The experience of tackling any extensive text should be a natural development, arising from previous explorations of pieces of dialogue in which the varying inflexions and layers of meaning that the words convey have been discovered through a process of weaving, in action and in stillness, a texture of sounds and silences.

It seems unfortunate that, too often, the study of dramatic texts is a sedentary process confined to the English department, while action and improvisation, often excluding the exploration of texts, belong to drama. English teachers may be contemptuous of action, drama teachers resentful of the dominance of academic attitudes to the word.

Suspicions apart, the argument put forward by teachers of English is, usually, that practical sessions take up more time than can be spared when a number of texts have to be studied. This is understandable but, if at least parts of one or two texts were to be explored in action (not, of course, anything approaching a production), it is likely that this process would help to develop the ability to read and penetrate other texts in depth. For example, when, in the second scene of the play, Hamlet responds to his mother's plea not to return to Wittenberg with:

> I shall in all my best
> Obey you Madam.

his stance and gestures, and his distance from his mother, not only reflect his immediate relationship with her, but serve as an indication on which to develop his future encounters with her.

> That moment is crucial to the direction of the play, and, in any actor's conception of the play, becomes primary. It's about mothers. It's about what she is doing as a woman to me as a man; and his relationship is to a woman, who is also his mother, and also to what he does next. That sort of insight may occur over a period of years. One may have deduced it, but may not have known it until one does it. It's got to be experienced; knowing that it's there, and will emerge – but the form that it will take, the voice that it will take – the actor does not know until he does it.[1]

[1] Neil Johnston – interview

This underlines much of what this book is about – knowing in the moment of doing and, because the process is the expressive one, knowing, in that moment, one's feelings in relationship to one's mother, and not merely that of Hamlet to *his* mother.

If, in drama sessions, there has been concern for the vivid communication of images then such passages as the tale of Falstaff's death:

'e'vn at the turning o'th Tyde'

'his Nose was as sharpe as a Pen'

'and all was as cold as any stone'

will come as from a veritable eye-witness. But the communication of this event depends not only on the vividness of the images, but also on the relationship (distance, stance, gestures) of the listeners. Experimentation with this relationship will reveal a number of versions of the episode. 'Distance has a feeling about it, just as closeness has a feeling about *it*'.[1] Experiments of this kind can add extra dimensions to the words.

PERFORMANCE

In schools there may be all sorts of occasions for showing work to another group. Such occasions may range from one where a parallel class is invited to be present, to one of performance to a public audience of some kind.

Any occasion of performance, however informal, involves a degree of exposure. If the children's resources have reached a sufficient depth for the quality of communication between them not to be disrupted, the experience may lend an edge to all that has gone before. If it is ill-timed it may be destructive. In a sense the ordinary drama sessions provide the kind of preparation which might be thought of as rehearsals, though not with performance in mind, while rehearsals which do have presentation in view need to be regarded as a process of growth and not merely occasions of preparation, under pressure, for a particular event. 'A director learns that the growth of rehearsals is a developing process; he sees that there is a right time for everything, and his art is the art of recognizing these moments.'[2]

Much depends on the way in which any audience (onlookers

[1] Leslie Read – interview
[2] *The Empty Space* by Peter Brook, MacGibbon & Kee

is perhaps a better term) is disposed in relation to the action. If the number is small, people can probably sit anywhere as long as they do not get in the way, but with a larger group (e.g. more than thirty) the relationship needs to be worked out.

> . . . for each production, a new space is designed for the actors and spectators. Thus, infinite variation of performer-audience relationships is possible. The actors can play among the spectators, directly contacting the audience and giving it a passive role in the drama. Or the actors may build structures among the spectators and thus include them in the architecture of action, subjecting them to a sense of pressure and congestion and limitation of space. Or the actors may play among the spectators and ignore them, looking through them.[1]

In one drama school for the training of professional actors the students gave their first performances in a space the size of a large classroom, and never, in the course of their training, performed to an audience of more than two hundred.

In some schools a public performance always rests on a dramatist's text, in others it is usually a version of a text or story with an improvised dialogue, and in some it is based entirely on improvisation round some theme. The decision rests, in part, on the availability of texts that are worth pursuing and which the children can make their own. It also depends on the nature of previous experience, the number to be involved and the balance between boys and girls.

There are schools and, especially, Youth Theatres where performance dominates and is not the outcome of growth; but one Youth Theatre in South London evolved differently:

> The reason was, in the first place, because we had the whole school building at our disposal, and we got together a whole group of people who were very varied, and committed to lots of things, not just drama. Every room in the school was used for various activities, such as photography, visual arts and so on; so drama became a social activity rather than linked with performance.
>
> But the work began to fragment a bit, so I decided that one way of bringing people together might be a

[1] *Towards a Poor Theatre* by Jerzy Grotowski, Methuen

performance. So we did *The Threepenny Opera*. I felt the
need for a script and for open possibilities of doing it –
projections, music and so on. The thing built up from
there so that we had 600 kids on the books. The performance
was a good catalyst, and afterwards we were able to work
fruitfully in the ordinary sessions. They began to understand
the resources they needed.[1]

Geoffrey Reeves has referred to theatre 'when it is exciting and
meaningful' as 'the heightened shaping of things', and while the
ordinary drama sessions may well have something of this quality,
performance (if it is timely) demands a heightened level of energy
and adds an edge to the experience.

If the nature of the 'play', the size and disposition of the
audience, emerge from previous work there is a valuable intensi-
fication of experience but no sudden change of direction.

DESIGN

As soon as the dimensions of a playing space and its relationship
to the audience are considered, an element of design is involved.
This holds even for such a simple situation as when one group
presents something that it has done to the rest of the class, or
when one class shows its work to another.

Alterations in the wearing of ordinary clothes – rolling up
sleeves or trouser legs, turning up a collar, buttoning up a jacket
or hanging it loosely over the shoulders – suggest elements of
costume; so also does the wearing of a hat or cap on the back of
the head, or tipped over one eye. Even such simple alterations,
involving changes of shape, weight and tightness or looseness of
garments have an impact not only on appearance, but on the
experience of oneself.

Further developments involve the use of different materials,
discrimination in the choice and blending of colours and the
understanding and manipulation of shapes. The impact of
different colours, and gradations of light on various shapes and
materials can be explored by the use of coloured slides, made and
projected by the children themselves. On one occasion life-size
hardboard cut-outs were made of each other by the actors, and
supported by struts so that they stood upright. The purpose of

[1] Roger Sell – interview

this preparatory exercise (for *The Winter's Tale*) was to focus attention on silhouettes as conveying the most immediately telling information about persons and characters.

Design demands the development of the ability to look – whether this involves the relationships between different colours, tones and textures, the shape of a jacket or of a tree (rather than the cliché of a tree) or, when a mask is to be made, the acute study of faces.

Much of this needs the continuing help of the art department, but if the time comes for the public presentation of a play there is much to be said for the actors themselves taking, under guidance, a full share in the evolution of all the elements of design. If they have been accustomed, from the earliest and simplest situations, to do this, they will have learnt that, as well as heightening ideas, design must be functional. Things have to be worn, handled, entered through, climbed upon, and design must not say too much so that nothing is left to the imagination of the spectators. 'You inhabit the world you are trying to create, and it is important that all concerned should inhabit the same world. This demands a high degree of understanding from *everybody* who is involved'.[1]

[1] Malcolm Pride – interview

Postscript

> There is no criticism, and the whole aim of the course is to equip people to grasp what they already possess.

This statement is not lifted, as might be supposed, from the prospectus of some educational establishment with an easy-going outlook; it is quoted from an article[1] by Irving Wardle, theatre critic of *The Times*, describing the Theatre Center at Dallas in the USA – 'a theatre that has to fill its seats to survive'. 'Quality apart (and some of the work was marvellous), the Centre's main claim is that of a theatrical power-house from which Britain, as well as the United States, has something to learn. . . . Paul Baker, the man responsible for the enterprise, is the Centre's founding director, but also Chairman of the Drama Department at Trinity University, San Antonio. Graduate students from Trinity go on to take a master's degree at Dallas. . . . The San Antonio-Dallas operation is not based on the aristocracy of talent. As a teacher, Baker assumes the creative potential of everyone who joins his class.'

'To grasp what they already possess' – that is to say to reveal to each individual resources never before réalised or used. This is a statement that echoes many made in previous chapters by directors, actors, choreographers, dancers and teachers. It is a capacity which is the hallmark of all great teachers whether in the professional or educational fields, whether those they work with are children, students, or experienced performers and whether slenderly, or greatly, gifted.

If each individual is to be helped to grasp that which, unknown to him, he already possesses, there can be no dependence upon a

[1] *The Times*, 18 June 1974

set of recipes, but only a series of guided searches, leading to unique discoveries. Hence the frequent use in previous chapters of the terms 'exploration' and 'process'.

While an emphasis on individual differences is inescapable the process of discovery is not necessarily a solitary one; much emerges in the give and take between one person and another.

Experience of ourselves springs from feeling which reverberates through our being and is manifested in action and attitude. Whether or not we are overwhelmed, or can command ourselves, depends upon whether we are able to recall, and so recognise, the impulses that stir us. This is only possible if we can express them in a medium – a medium that may be words (spoken or written), sound, colour, clay or movement. Of these sound and movement are the most intimate and immediate, and, therefore, peculiarly potent.

Feeling is inherent in everything that we do, but it is in expressive acts that it is both deepened and controlled. This process is served by the arts.

That which we know in our bones is knowing that has been absorbed into the fabric of our being. It underlies our attitudes, our awareness of ourselves, and of the world that we inhabit.

APPENDIX

Dance at the High School of Art, Manchester

In a Northern industrial city, in a desolate area opposite the gaol, there is a school in a building which, though not prisonlike, looks as if it belonged to the same grim period of architecture. Inside, since it is a High School of Art, considerable efforts have been made to civilise the building, but glass partitions between the classrooms and round both halls make the most of any noise. This creates problems for everybody.

In a long narrow hall, with eight doorways to classrooms or corridors, the girls dance. They dance throughout their school career, from eleven to eighteen years, with remarkable confidence. The presence of a stranger does not disturb them in any way, neither do they lose their absorption when, as often happens, the hall is invaded both during and at the end of a period.

Classes usually last for a double period, thus there is time for the girls to get going in action after the sedentary work in the classroom and, very importantly, there is also the time which is so necessary if the imagination is to be stirred and set to work. From the third year upwards those who are particularly interested in dance have the option of extra time, and at the top of the school the girls who offer dance for C.S.E. have five periods on the programme but also do a good deal of work beyond this.

The girls change, under very great difficulties, into leotards and, many of them, into tights. Most of them choose dark colours, but there is an occasional flashing red and when this is worn by a tall, attenuated coloured girl the impact is tremendous. They work barefoot, disregarding the inevitably dirty floor.

Work starts as soon as the girls come into the hall, even though traffic may still be passing through. The lesson begins with a brief introductory phase of movement training directed by the teacher; this is likely to be related generally to the needs of the next stage. Soon an idea involving composition, usually in small groups or in pairs, is introduced by the teacher and developed by the girls. A word, a piece of sculpture, an abstract design shown on a coloured slide or a piece of music may be the starting point. The teacher says that she tried 'to use as many ways into dance as possible, not just to stress the movement things. To try to use all their senses, to stimulate a response so that they use their eyes and ears'. They go to the Lake District or Snowdonia for weekends when they paint and write as well as dance, and these experiences feed their work when they are back at school.

The teacher observes the girls very closely as they work, and by her comments helps them to develop their ideas. Every girl can count on her individual attention and help, and thus know that she is known.

Sometimes each of the developing compositions is watched intently by the whole class. Their comments are perceptive and constructive to an unusual degree. Sometimes they repeat, with obvious pleasure, a previously completed piece, and sometimes individuals, a pair or a group present the compositions they have worked on independently in their spare time.

These spare-time compositions are developed during the dinner hour or after school, whenever the girls can secure a space in the hall and, if they need music, get a turn with the record player. The initiative lies with the girls; their involvement and persistence in the face of considerable difficulties are of a kind that one usually associates with boys and football.

The compositions are worked out very thoroughly, they are very varied, and a surprising number emerge at all age levels.

Some of the statements the girls have made about dance and which point to reasons for their involvement:

Age 15 I dance because it is an excellent way of describing how you feel, which is not possible in any other way. I find it an easier way of communicating with people. I tend to express things in much more detail, finding every aspect of it. Dancing makes you think more deeply about what you are doing. You seem to be able to get lost in a world of your own.

Age 16 I want to dance because I feel that I can express my ideas more freely and explicitly. I like to move with a feeling that I am putting over my ideas plainly and expressing them so that everybody can understand them.

Age 15 Dance makes me feel free to express whatever I feel at that time into movement.

Age 17 (A girl with considerable problems at home and who, before she began to dance $2\frac{1}{2}$ years ago, had been in constant trouble at school, even to the point of being suspended.)
Dance means a lot to me, it holds a future. I can express myself in dance when I can't express myself in speech or writing. Dance holds many dimensions I can't go into. Only the feelings it gives me.

Age 15 Dance seems to open my mind to everything. I also seem to be able to look at an object and dance to it. I can also say what I mean more clearly.

From these comments, and there are many more of a similar nature, it seems clear that in dance the girls find an opportunity for coming to terms with themselves in a way which is deeply satisfying. They stress that it is a process of clarification. Though they are concerned with their own feelings their compositions are not self-indulgent. In a strict sense their work is not highly developed technically, but what they do is clear and self-commanding; feeling and form are a unity.

The headmaster, Ernest Goodman (himself a specialist in the visual arts), spoke of the impact of dance 'on a whole group of disaffected girls in the Middle School, many with very serious home problems. They were problem girls; I don't mean they were vicious, they were disaffected, and the change in attitude was remarkable in quite a short space of time. It isn't just that they danced well and were happy in their dance. They began to be more co-operative, they wanted to be involved in all sorts of ways, and they became gentler people'. He went on – 'I feel that something very important is happening to them and I'm not awfully sure what it is, but it certainly must involve a discovery of personal powers, a discovery of one's uniqueness. To my mind no social integration, no happy relationships, can be developed without this'.[1]

From time to time the work is shown outside the school. One such occasion was a Spring Festival at a school on a housing estate on the outskirts of Manchester. It was a very difficult occasion. The audience was seated round three sides of a rectangle, and consisted for the most part of mothers with their understandably restless young children, schoolchildren and older boys whose main interest appeared to be in the revealing tights and leotards worn by the girls. There were other items, and the evening soon became too long and too late, and the audience did not necessarily wait until the end of a dance before leaving. This audience was clearly baffled by what it was looking at; for the audience the word dance stood for something quite different from what the girls were doing; but if a composition appealed to them they cheered rather as if they were at a football match. The girls, who were drawn from every part of the school, did not allow themselves to be discomposed and it was impressive to see individuals and groups take command of the awkward space and put everything they had got into an effort to hold the attention of their audience.

On another occasion, a group of 5th and 6th Form girls studying *Macbeth* for 'O' level evolved a danced version of the play. Their first rehearsal in an auditorium, which was also their first experience of working on a stage, was not easy. They had to place the action in a wide, shallow space, and while they moved through the pattern of the action an inexperienced group of boys experimented with the lighting so that the dancers sometimes found themselves blacked out, and often subject to violent changes of light. They did not turn a hair.

The rehearsal proper then started and altogether lasted from 2 p.m. to 5.15 p.m. with a short break. The dancers never lost their concentration or dropped the level of vitality. Their attitude was professional, in the best sense.

They had not solved the difficulties of combining speaking and dancing which occasionally they attempted to do, and since they

[1] Ernest Goodman – interview

were all girls they were more at home as witches than as warriors, and Macbeth had to work hard to sustain a male element. Surprisingly, however, one was seldom aware that these were all girls.

Altogether it was a remarkable achievement developed and sustained at a length which is not very usual in the field of dance.

In all that they do these girls manifest a degree of involvement and a level of vitality which ought to be, but often seems not to be, characteristic of youth.

One of the things Ernest Goodman said was, 'What impressed me quite early in watching them dance was how much more beautiful the girls seemed when they were involved in dancing; even very young girls looked, suddenly, beautiful when they moved.'

There were no ugly ducklings.

How much of this achievement is brought about by a gifted, concerned and generous teacher? How much by the attitude to the arts in this school? How much because dance is the medium?

As so often in education there are no answers to these questions because all these, and other elements, are interwoven. In dance, however, the person is both instrument and medium, so success is very potent, while failure is felt as disastrous.

This series of photographs shows some of the work done in dance by the girls at the High School of Art, Manchester. Every 'year', from the first (12 years) to the fifth (16 years) is included, but not in that order.

Booklist

The Intelligence of Feeling by Robert W. Witkin, Heinemann
Educational Books
The Principles of Art by R. G. Collingwood, Oxford University
Press
Phenomenology of Perception by Merlau-Ponty, Routledge &
Kegan Paul
Problems of Art by Susanne K. Langer, Routledge & Kegan Paul
Feeling and Form by Susanne K. Langer, Routledge & Kegan Paul
The Aims of Education by A. N. Whitehead, Benn
Language and Learning by James Britton, Allen Lane
The Seamless Web by S. Burnshaw, Allen Lane
The Empty Space by Peter Brook, MacGibbon & Kee
Towards a Poor Theatre by Jerzy Grotowski, Methuen
Orghast at Persepolis edited by A. C. H. Smith, Methuen
Voice and the Actor by Cicely Berry, Harrap